W9-CBK-066

LIVING CHURCH BOOKS

some titles in this series

Christianity and Communism Today
John C. Bennett

Pro-Existence: Christian Voices in East Germany
edited by Elisabeth Adler

Servants of God in People's China
Katharine Hockin

Christians and Power Politics
Alan Booth

DONALD EVANS

Communist Faith and Christian Faith

SCM PRESS
BLOOMSBURY STREET LONDON

NOTE

This book, although written by Professor Donald Evans of the University of Toronto, was adopted as a report of the Committee on Christian Faith of the United Church of Canada, and was given general approval by the twenty-first General Council, September 1964.

FIRST BRITISH EDITION 1965

© THE RYERSON PRESS, TORONTO, 1964

PRINTED IN GREAT BRITAIN BY
NORTHUMBERLAND PRESS LIMITED
GATESHEAD

261.73
Ev9

PREFACE

At the Nineteenth General Council of the United Church of Canada the following resolution was passed:

'Be it resolved that the Nineteenth General Council direct its Committee on Christian Faith to study the nature and practice of communism as a faith and way of life and as an eschatological hope; produce a statement setting forth the Christian faith and practice over against those communist hopes and claims; advise the Church concerning practical programmes and valid attitudes in its world-wide mission and at home; prepare a study booklet in this area, designed for use in youth and lay groups within the Church; and report to the Twentieth General Council.'

The Committee on Christian Faith has produced a statement in the form of a study booklet on Communist faith and Christian faith. We have not tried to provide detailed advice concerning 'practical programmes and attitudes' for Christians everywhere, since such programmes and attitudes differ greatly for Christians in different situations. We would not presume to offer a common formula for a Christian trade-unionist in Sudbury, a Christian missionary in Brazil, and a Christian teacher in East Germany. But we do hope that this booklet will indicate some of the fundamental issues which are involved, and thus be a useful guide for Christians who encounter Communism in varied situations.

We also hope that readers will be stimulated to pursue the issues further by exploring some of the best literature on Christianity and Communism. In this area the lament of Ecclesiastes is especially appropriate: 'Of making many books there is no end'. Some of the studies are extremely good, however. We have appended two bibliographies which we recommend. The first is a brief list of elementary works which would be helpful in study groups. The second is a longer list for those who wish to probe more deeply into the subject.

The preliminary work for this document was done by a committee led by Dr A. C. Forrest. In its present form, however, it is entirely the work of Professor D. D. Evans who has devoted enormous labour and great talent to the production of a document which is intended not to express his own views but to be

37392

acceptable to the Committee as a whole. He has revised and re-written the document—in some places more than once—to take account of the Committee's criticism. The Committee then accepts full responsibility for the Report in its present form, but recognizes that the credit for any merits it may have belongs largely to Professor Evans.

For this edition, Professor Evans has received permission to add some footnotes (which bear his initials) and a postscript. These personal additions are not part of the report which was given general approval by the 21st General Council of the United Church of Canada.

D. M. MATHERS
Chairman
J. R. HORD
Secretary

CONTENTS

INTRODUCTION

Christians have convictions. Communists have convictions. This study booklet is a comparison.

In relation to the Christian faith, Communist convictions can be divided into three groups: those which a Christian should reject, those which a Christian should accept, and those which a Christian is free either to accept or to reject.

Which Communist convictions belong to which group? Concerning some, Christians generally would give the same answer. For example, most Christians would agree concerning where to place the Communist denial of God, the Communist concern for the poor, and the Communist claim that a capitalist economy has inherent contradictions:

A Christian should *reject* Communist atheism, although he may agree with many Communist criticisms of religion.

A Christian should *accept* Communist concern for the poor and powerless in so far as it resembles the divine concern which is revealed throughout the Bible.

A Christian is *free* either to accept or to reject the Communist account of economic processes which are at work in modern capitalism. A Christian is 'free' in the sense that his faith does not dictate answers to factual questions in economics. If he accepts or rejects Communist answers to such questions, it is because these answers do or do not square with the facts.

Often, however, Christians do not agree as to what their attitude should be towards a particular Communist conviction. Indeed, there is sometimes more than disagreement among Christians; there is confusion and even suspicion. Some Christians seem to accept almost everything in Communism, whereas others seem to reject almost everything. We hope that this report will help such Christians—and the vast majority who stand somewhere in between—to understand one another. Nevertheless, our attempt to understand the varied views of Christians has not led us to 'sit on the fence' ourselves. Wherever there has been general agreement in the Committee, we have set forth our own considered opinion concerning which Communist convictions should be rejected, which should be accepted, and which are optional. Of course, we do not expect everyone else to agree with us, and we are not presuming to 'lay down the law' for individual Christians. But we feel that our study will be more useful as a basis for discussion and reflection if we express our findings clearly and simply. We hope that this will not be misinterpreted as dogmatism.

We should make it clear, right from the start, that we are not comparing Christianity and Communism by comparing life in the 'Christian West' with life in Communist Russia or Communist China. There are three reasons for not doing this. First, such a comparison requires extensive sociological research which is not within the scope and competence of a Committee on Christian Faith. Second, and more important, we are not willing to equate the Christian faith with what goes on in Western Europe and North America. The Christian faith is not the same thing as organized Christianity, and organized Christianity itself does not deserve either the credit for all that is good in Western society or the blame for all that is bad. Third, we think that Christians will fail to understand the appeal and the challenge of Communism if we do not distinguish its ideals from its practices, its goals from its achievements, its convictions from its results. Indeed, if a Communist should try to understand the appeal and challenge of the Christian faith he would need to make use of a similar distinction. It is true that a Communist and a Christian each insists that his theory and practice ought to coincide; but it would be rash to assume that they do coincide. Moreover, even where a Communist dogma or a Christian dogma is not fully believed or fully applied, it is an important element in the total situation. It forms part of the framework within which a Communist or a Christian interprets his situation and acts in the world. Just as any understanding of Christianity requires at least a rudimentary knowledge of Christian theology, so an understanding of Communism requires a rudimentary knowledge of Marxism-Leninism, its official theory.

Our task, then, is not to compare life under Communist rule with life in the so-called 'Christian West'. Rather, it is to compare the basic convictions of Communist and Christian, convictions concerning fundamentals:

(a) nature, man and God
(b) economics and property
(c) history, hope and morality

Readers should realize that such an approach, however useful it may be, has its limitations. Communism is not merely a set of convictions; it is a powerful political movement of men who rule one-third of the human race and who plot revolution throughout the rest of the world. A comprehensive survey of Communism would describe Communist practice in detail. Since we have not tried to do this, readers should consult one of the excellent surveys which are listed in the bibliographies.

Our task is to compare Communist faith and Christian faith. Even this limited objective may seem wrong-headed to some Christians. 'How can you undertake any comparison between the convictions of Communist and Christian?' they may ask. 'A Communist has faith in an ideology, in Marxism; but a Christian has faith in a person, in Jesus Christ. How can you compare belief in a system of ideas with trust in a person?'

To this we can only answer, 'Your objection is important, and there is much truth in it; but you exaggerate. On the one hand, it is true that Christian faith is primarily a trust in a person; but it also includes various ideas which may conflict or harmonize with the main ideas in Marxism. On the other hand, it is true that Communist faith is primarily a belief in a system of Marxist ideas; but the convictions of a Communist involve attitudes which may conflict or harmonize with those of the Christian faith; loyalty to the Party, trust in economic forces, hope for a better life on earth, self-sacrifice on behalf of others. If Christian faith and Communist faith were so unlike that they could not even be compared, then it would be impossible for them either to conflict or to agree concerning anything. This is not the case.'

Christians and Communists live in the same world and will continue to do so for many years. Their relations to each other are more complex and varied than North Americans are apt to suppose. It may well prove, indeed, that the most urgent question for Christians is not how to meet Communism but how to meet Communists.

Christians and Communists meet under a great variety of circumstances. In North America, where Christianity is generally respected if not always practised, the most conspicuous problem is that of foreign relations: Should Christians press for mutual understanding with Communist nations, or should the cold war be regarded as a sort of crusade? In countries under Communist rule, Christians must determine the nature and extent of the loyalty they owe to the state. In many parts of Asia and Africa, where Christians and Communists have a common antipathy to colonialism, the encounter takes a different form again.

In this report we have kept in mind the urgent, practical questions of Christians who encounter Communists in these varying situations; but we have not tried to provide specific answers to their questions. We have not provided answers concerning nuclear arms, Communist-state loyalty oaths, or anti-colonial revolutions. We hope, however, that this study booklet along with some of the reports and books listed in the bibliography will help to provide a basis for Christian decisions which are reasonable and faithful.

In our account of Communist convictions we have selected those which are generally shared by Communists today, ignoring those which are not. Some of the differences between Communists today are very important in international relations. The dispute between Russia and China is an obvious example. On the whole, however, the differences are not very important in a comparison between Communist faith and Christian faith. We have only indicated some of them in footnotes.

Our study is restricted to contemporary Communist convictions because Communist theory has changed considerably since it began with Karl Marx in the 1840's. Some of Marx's most interesting ideas of 1844 do not form part of Communist theory today. We shall not consider Marx in himself, but Marx as he is interpreted by contemporary Communism.

We are interested in the common core of Communist convictions. Such a core exists and is unlikely to disappear in the near future. It is true that Communists differ, Communists change in convictions and Communists vary enormously in their degree of conviction and their dedication to the cause. These complex differences, changes and variations form part of the concrete situation in which Christians live today. But so also does the common core of Communist theory, which is our focus of interest in this study booklet.

Before we consider Communist faith and Christian faith, however, we shall briefly outline the historical movements which lie behind them: Communism and Christianity.

1

Communism and Christianity

ORIGINS

Communism had its origin within western civilization, which had been shaped by Judaism and Christianity. Communists vehemently reject many aspects of western civilization; but some Christians maintain that so much of the Communist philosophy and social outlook has been derived from Judaeo-Christian sources that Communism is really a 'Christian heresy'. Typical features of this inheritance are Communism's intense concern for social justice, its expectation of a meaningful culmination of history and its conception of a leavening group of dedicated men who transform society from within. Since Communism arose partly because such this-worldly features of the Christian faith had been neglected by Christians, it has sometimes been viewed as a 'divine judgment' on Christendom.

Christianity had its origin within Judaism, from which it inherited the moral teaching of the law and the prophets and its conception of the church as a people chosen by God to receive his life and to communicate it to the world. Christians accept the basic Jewish beliefs concerning God and morality, but they reject most of the regulations which govern the Jewish religious community. Christianity originated in the life, death and resurrection of Jesus Christ, for whom Christians claim universal authority.

SCRIPTURES

Communists accept certain documents as authoritative. Two such documents are universally regarded as primary: the

Communist Manifesto, published in 1848 by Karl Marx and Friedrich Engels, and *Capital*, begun by Marx and completed after his death by Engels. The writings of V. I. Lenin, the first leader of the Soviet Union, are venerated almost as much. The authority of these documents rests solely on the belief in their inherent value and not on any theory of their infallibility. In practice the authority is unquestioned, although over the years there have been important changes in emphasis and even in interpretation.

Christians accept certain documents as authoritative. These are the Jewish sacred scriptures (Old Testament) and the distinctively Christian writings (New Testament). Many Christians also accept the Jewish writings known as Apocrypha, and some denominations add very considerably to the list of authoritative documents. Christians also differ in their definition of the authority of scripture, but all agree that the Bible's witness to Jesus Christ makes it essential to faith.

GROUP ORGANIZATION

Although he took an active part in a workers' organization known as the 'First International', Marx believed that his function was to provide theoretical ammunition for the working class as a whole. The Communist Party as we know it today is largely the work of Lenin, who believed that conditions in Czarist Russia required a tightly disciplined and indoctrinated Marxist group. When the Czarist regime was overthrown by liberal democrats, it was the Leninist group known as the 'Bolsheviks' with their centralized control which eventually attained power. The Communist Party in Russia is not a mass organization but has remained a group of the elite, a small officers' group which is subject to central authority.

Although during his life on earth Jesus launched no big-scale movement, he gathered an intimate group of disciples for instruction and fellowship. When he was crucified his followers scattered; but they came together again after the Resurrection. Later at Pentecost they received the gift of the Holy Spirit and the power to go forth to proclaim the Gospel to the world. A theology for the world mission of the Church was initiated by St Paul, a convert from Judaism who became the apostle to the Gentiles. The Church has regarded itself as an open society, inviting all into its membership on the sole condition of faith. In principle all members are expected to participate fully in both the worship and witness of the Church; but in practice a professional clergy has often ministered to a largely passive laity.

GROUP DISCIPLINE AND ORTHODOXY

Communists refer to their common convictions as 'Marxism-Leninism', a 'system of philosophical, economic and socio-political views' endorsed by the Party. This system provides an orthodoxy from which Communists are not permitted to deviate. At any particular time, however, some issues concerning theory or practice are open to free discussion within the Party. Nevertheless, once a decision has been reached, Party members must give it complete and unquestioning support. The 'party line' is often designed to cope in a practical way with a particular situation of the moment, and it may suddenly change if circumstances or Party leadership change; yet it is as obligatory as the central tenets of Marxism-Leninism.

Christian churches vary tremendously in the extent to which they demand adherence to the decisions of a central organization. In the Roman Catholic Church the Pope is held to be infallible when on rare occasions he speaks *ex cathedra* (that is, with the deliberate intention of officially proclaiming dogma concerning faith and morals); also, church authority over ritual and church law is highly centralized. Protestant communions make no claim to infallibility but they do require candidates for membership to make a credible profession of the Christian faith and to acknowledge a discipline in their lives. All churches admit that many matters of faith and action are open to free discussion and individual judgment; but even the most liberal groups have a minimal orthodoxy.

PROBLEMS OF UNITY

After the Russian revolution of 1917, the Communist Party throughout the world came to be dominated by the Russian Party. An impressive united front was presented to the world; whenever the party line changed at Moscow, all Communist Parties followed, and any individual Communists who disagreed either conformed quickly or disappeared from the ranks. In 1948, however, the Yugoslav Communist Party under Marshal Tito established its independence from Moscow; and since 1963 the Communist Parties of China and Russia have been disagreeing vehemently in public. These schisms have detracted considerably from the cohesion of the Communist bloc; they remind us that Marxist principles do not of themselves guarantee an unbreakable unity.

In spite of dissenting movements which appeared almost from the beginning, the majority of Christians maintained close communion with one another for several centuries. In the fifth century, however, two large groups broke away in the near east. In 1054 a growing lack of sympathy between Greek and Latin sections of the Church led to a further rupture, separating Greek Orthodox from Roman Catholics. Luther's movement to reform the Roman Catholic Church in the sixteenth century resulted in still another split, and the Protestantism which emerged has undergone a continuous process of division. In our century, however, the trend has reversed. Protestants have united in such movements as The United Church of Canada, Protestant and Orthodox communions have co-operated in the World Council of Churches, and the Second Vatican Council has led to improved relations between Roman Catholics and other Christians.

2

Nature, Man and God

What does the Communist Believe about Nature, Man and God?

Material Factors are primary

Communist convictions concerning nature, man and God are based on the 'historical materialism' of Marx and Engels. Marx and Engels taught that the fundamental factors in human life are 'material'; that is, they are *economic*.

Communists describe these economic factors in a technical language which must be understood by anyone who wishes to understand Communism. We hope that readers will study the next few pages very carefully, for they are the most difficult and the most fundamental.

Historical materialism maintains that the economic basis of a society, on which all else depends, has two main elements: 'forces' of production and 'relations' of production.

1. *Forces of Production* (or 'productive forces') are three-fold:
   (a) *Objects* of labour—*natural resources* (e.g., virgin land)
   —*raw materials* (that is, natural resources which men have already worked on, e.g., cultivated land, seeds or bricks).
   (b) *Instruments* of labour—tools or machines or factories.
   (c) *Men* who labour—their needs and their skills (Note that the term 'means of production', which will be used later, refers to (a) and (b) together.)

2. *Relations of production* depend on *ownership* of forces of production, and give each society its economic system or

power-structure. Communists distinguish five kinds of economic system:

(i) *Primitive Communism.* Common ownership of the objects of labour and of the few instruments which exist.
(ii) *Ancient Slavery.* A ruling class of masters owns all the forces of production, including the men who labour. The slaves own nothing.
(iii) *Medieval Feudalism.* A ruling class of lords owns most of the means of production, but not the men who labour. The latter, called 'serfs', are nevertheless tied to the land, lacking full ownership of their own labour power.
(iv) *Bourgeois Capitalism.* A ruling class of capitalists owns all the means of production. The industrial working class or 'proletariat' owns its own labour power, but none of the means of production.
(v) *Socialism and Communism.* Common ownership of the means of production.

According to historical materialism, the history of mankind has conformed to objective laws of economic change. Changes in the forces of production bring about changes in the relations of production. However, the latter tend to lag behind the former. That is, the economic power-structure tends to remain the same, even when new forces of production have made it obsolete; a new power structure emerges only after a period of conflict. For example, in sixteenth and seventeenth century England there were new forces of production: new natural resources became available, new technology was devised, and new labour skills were developed. These new productive forces formed a new mode of production which could not operate freely and effectively in the existing feudal system of ownership. The feudal relations of production had been appropriate for the agricultural and handicraft forces of production during medieval times, but they had become obsolete. A new class, the capitalists, engaged in class struggle with the feudal ruling class, and eventually emerged victorious. Today there is a new conflict: between the new industrial mode of production and the obsolete capitalist relations of production. This conflict is resolved only by the establishment of new relations of production. Private (capitalist) ownership of the means of production must be replaced by public ownership.

Historical materialism sees history as a series of class struggles: slave owners were displaced by a feudal aristocracy which in turn was displaced by a capitalist bourgeoisie. These ruling classes were minorities in society; but the new one, the 'proletariat', includes most of the people in a modern industrial state. According to Communist theory, when this class gains power so that 'socialism' is achieved, there will be no more exploitation of one class; no longer will one class derive income from the labour of another class merely by virtue of owning the means of production. Eventually 'socialism' will evolve into 'communism', a completely classless society. The state, which has been the instrument of class domination, will wither away. Men will no longer be alienated from one another but will become new social beings, working together harmoniously for the good of all. Men will no longer be alienated from the products of their own labour, which has been the property of other men; instead, they will express themselves freely and creatively in their daily work. Men will no longer be, in their own eyes and the eyes of others, mere commercial commodities; men will become masters of the economic laws which have hitherto determined their history. Communism will be 'the ascent of man from the kingdom of necessity to the kingdom of freedom' (Engels).

Communists contrast their historical materialism with all '*idealistic*' views of man and of human history. An idealistic view is one which claims that social changes and political revolutions originate in the 'consciousness' of man—that is, in the ideas and ideals of individuals or groups. Communists hold that the economic basis of any society determines its political, legal and social organization, and its ideas concerning politics, law, philosophy and God. These ideas may seem to be independent and powerful, but they are merely reflections of the underlying economic power-structure in society. The political, legal, philosophical and religious ideas of men at any particular time in history are merely a 'superstructure' which is thrown up from economic foundations. The system of ideas is merely an 'ideology', a 'false consciousness' which seems true to men in the ruling class merely because it supports their own economic self-interest. If an individual man sets forth some new ideas and ideals and these are actually accepted and applied in society, his success depends not on any overwhelming power which ideas have in themselves, but on underlying economic changes which necessitate this change in ideology. For example, historical materialists believe that Wilberforce was successful against slavery only because the slave-system was becoming obsolete as a relation of production in Britain because of new forces of production.

The dynamic structure of society as seen by historical materialism may be represented by a diagram.

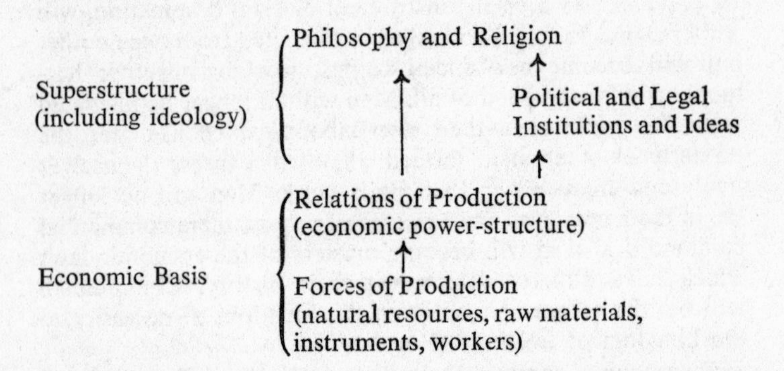

Engels pointed out that, although economic factors are decisive, various elements in the superstructure may react back on the economic basis; economic factors are the *ultimate* determinants, but not the *only* determinants, of change. (Hence the arrows in our diagram sometimes would point downwards.) For example, legal institutions depend primarily on relations of production or economic power-structure, but they may react back on the relations of production, modifying them, because they influence the distribution of property. Nevertheless, economic factors are primary and decisive. They govern the general processes of history, dominating human life like the relentless currents of a vast river. The historical materialism of Communists and other Marxists is opposed to all 'idealistic' views which hold that the superstructure is primary.

Communists believe that since their own ideas reflect the fundamental economic realities of our era, the eventual success of the Party is assured, and that since their ideology alone provides genuine knowledge of these realities it alone is genuinely 'scientific'. People who have other ideas are merely unrealistic 'idealists', whose ideas run counter to the inexorable movements of history. We should note that the Communist attack on 'idealism' is directed not only at non-Marxists but also at Marxists who accept the basic ideas of historical materialism but not the Leninist version of it. Lenin claimed for the Communist Party a unique authority in discerning and shaping the detailed processes of history.

Historical materialism, especially in its Communist form, is opposed to any *liberal* view of man as an individual who has rights today by virtue of his membership in the human race. Only when communism comes will the individual have value and dignity in himself, as a man; meanwhile, he is to be understood and dealt with as a member of a *class*. The only people who have any rights now are those who either belong to the working class or identify themselves with the interests of that class as interpreted by the Party. Everyone else is a class enemy; there is no appeal to his rights as a human being, for the notion of 'humanity' is a mere abstraction. During the 'socialist' stage of development, class enemies are dealt with severely and liberalism is a dangerous deviation. (This 'socialism' differs radically from that of the liberal Social Democrats, whom Communists generally regard as their greatest enemies.[1])

Historical materialism is opposed to any *mechanistic* theory

[1] In 1965, many Communists are conciliatory towards Social Democracy. Is this merely a tactical and temporary shift in the Communist Party 'line', as has so often been the case in the past? Or is it part of a fundamental and irreversible trend in Communist theory? I do not know. (D. E.)

in which men are placed on the same level as stones or machines and understood in the same way as inanimate nature. Man differs from nature in two ways. First, men have a history in which they gradually achieve mastery over nature; they achieve this mastery as they come to know what forces are at work in nature. Second, men will eventually achieve mastery over their own history; this will happen when they apply Marxist knowledge concerning the forces at work in history so as to bring in the classless society. Modern scientific knowledge concerning nature and history enables man to create his own future, his own destiny. Prometheus, the ancient mythical figure who stole fire from the gods for the welfare of mankind, is the symbolic hero of Marxism.

On the other hand, although man's creative or 'spiritual' powers are emphasized, historical materialism is opposed to any spiritualizing of nature. Matter itself is not alive, and not mental or spiritual. Rather, it has within itself the capacity to produce the life of organisms and of men. In other words, quantitative changes in matter can create qualitatively new beings. Matter itself is eternally material and eternally in motion. According to Engels, 'We have the certainty that matter remains eternally the same, and that none of its attributes can ever be lost.'

Communists believe that the root of moral evil, its decisive cause, is private ownership of the means of production. They also believe that the decisive remedy to moral evil is the proletarian revolution, which establishes social ownership of the means of production. These fundamental Communist convictions will be expounded more fully in chapters 3 and 4.

Religion is made by man

Communists are atheists. They hold that atheism is a natural and inescapable part of Marxism. Some followers of Marx separate his atheism from the rest of Marxism, but Communists do not. Indeed, they *base* their atheism on the historical materialism of Marx and Engels. They deny the existence of God and they criticize religion (including the Christian religion) in four different ways:

(i) Religion at its best is a well-meaning but *unrealistic idealism*, which foolishly seeks to remedy the alienation of men from one another and from nature by trying to change the inner consciousness of men without changing the economic power-structure. Since the consciousness of men is determined by this power-structure, religious idealism is futile and misguided. Men will remain alienated from one another until they all share in economic power and in the fruits of human mastery over nature. Marxist realism devotes its energies to bringing in the classless society, for the ultimate causes of evil in the world are economic, not personal.

(ii) Religion at its best is a *false fantasy* by which man cheats and deceives himself. Men create 'God' in their own image; that is, they gather together their ideas of unrealized human perfections and imagine that all these perfections already exist in one superhuman being called 'God'. Man deceives himself, worshipping his own being without understanding what he is doing. Man robs himself of his own intrinsic dignity by ascribing all his own virtue and worth to a fictitious God.

This notion of 'God', the imaginary realization of a true humanity, may have been useful as a vision of human possibilities for men who have been dehumanized in class-conflict societies. But in the classless society of the future, human possibilities can be realized, and there will be no need for 'God'.

(iii) Religion, more commonly, is an *evil illusion*. It is an 'opium' which the ruling classes provide for those whom they oppress so as to induce resignation and thus prevent revolution. Religion works like a drug, enabling miserable men to find an illusory escape from the oppressions and suffering of this world by dreaming of a better one: 'pie in the sky when you die'. In all previous societies there has been a use and a need for religion; it has been a necessary evil. In the classless 'communistic' society, however, there will be no use for it as an instrument of class domination, since there will be no classes; and there will be no need for it as an illusory satisfaction, since the mass of the people will enjoy an abundance of this-worldly goods and an opportunity for self-expression in creative work.

Meanwhile, however, Marx held that 'the abolition of religion as the illusory happiness of the people is required for their real happiness' (*On Religion,* page 42). People who dream of another world after death will not be inclined to change *this* world. Marx had a special contempt for the Christian religion as he observed it in nineteenth-century Germany and England. He held that it not only provides an opium for the proletariat, but also inculcates a submissive, helpless and servile attitude; moreover, it gives divine sanction to the authority of the oppressive ruling class. Lenin held that religion has a function for the ruling class: 'As for those who live upon the labour of others, religion teaches them to be charitable in earthly life, thus providing a cheap justification for their whole exploiting existence and selling them, at a reasonable price, tickets to heavenly bliss' (*Religion,* p. 7).

(iv) Religion is not only unrealistic, self-deceptive and anti-revolutionary; it is also a false substitute for science. It is *pseudo-science.* The Communist, like some non-Marxist unbelievers in the West, held that religion is a pseudo-science which arises from man's fear of uncontrollable forces; religion is gradually being displaced by genuine science.

'It is necessary to explain patiently the untenability of religious beliefs, which were engendered in the past when people were overawed by the elemental forces and social oppression and did not know the real causes of natural and social phenomena. This can be done by making use of the achievements of modern science, which steadily solves the mysteries of the universe and extends man's power over nature, leaving no room for religious inventions about supernatural forces' (1961 Programme of the Communist Party of the Soviet Union).

'Science, on the Marxist view, has driven mystery out of nature; it has now only to be turned by man upon his own society in order to drive mystery out of this sphere also, and to place social phenomena under man's purposive control. When this process has been completed, it will have removed, according to Marxian analysis, the bases of religion. Religion is based upon man's awe for what he does not understand and on his impotence before forces which he cannot control. He personifies these forces and worships them. Science ends his impotence and with it the possibility of worship, for he cannot worship what is within his control' (M. B. Foster, *Christian Faith and Communist Faith,* p. 95. Foster, a Christian expounding Marxism, goes on to disagree).

Only atheism is rational

We have seen that the Communist's denial of God's existence depends partly on his explanations of the origins of religious belief. Religion is a false fantasy in which man creates God in the ideal image of himself. Religion is an evil illusion which arises because man hopes for God and heaven as an escape from suffering and oppression. Religion occurs where men fear uncontrollable forces and do not yet have a scientific explanation which enables them to gain control.

Communists, along with non-Communist atheists in the West, also set forth other arguments in support of atheism:

1. The existence of God cannot be proved by observation (the astronauts did not see him!), or by scientific experiment, or by strict logic.
2. The world is eternal. Since it had no beginning, there is no need to infer a world-Creator. Therefore there is no world-Creator.
3. Whatever is immaterial (for example, human ideas) always depends on something material. Therefore, God, who is supposed to be immaterial and independent of matter, cannot exist.
4. Man is the source of his own existence as man rather than beast, for human history is 'nothing more than the development of man through human labour and the development of nature for man' (Marx). Hence there is no need to infer a Creator of man.
5. Jesus of Nazareth, on whom Christians depend so much for their faith in God, probably did not even exist.

In place of a faith in God, Communists advocate a faith in *man*:

The power and rationality of man	'Man can and will understand everything, and in his development can achieve everything necessary for the progress of society' (Duncker).
The supremacy of man	'The criticism of religion ends with the precept that the supreme being for man is man' (Marx).
The divinity of man	Prometheus 'the noblest of saints and martyrs' hated all gods who did not acknowledge the 'consciousness of man as the supreme divinity' (Marx).

Religion can and must be eliminated

Communists are committed to a two-pronged attack on religion: proletarian revolution and atheistic education. The first is an indirect attack, but in their eyes it is more important.

Proletarian revolution is essential because religion is part of the ideological superstructure of capitalism and it will only disappear when its economic basis has been destroyed. Lenin held that although religion arose originally from a fear of apparently uncontrollable forces in *nature*, its primary basis now is a fear of uncontrollable forces in capitalist *society*. 'The roots of modern religion are deeply embedded in the social oppression of the working masses, and in their apparently complete helplessness before the blind forces of capitalism' (*Religion,* p. 14). Hence it is unrealistic idealism to suppose that atheistic education by itself could eliminate religion. The masses must first learn 'to fight against the social facts from which religion arises' (p. 15). In 1905 Lenin insisted that religious believers should not be excluded from participation in revolutionary activity. 'The unity of the genuinely revolutionary struggle of the oppressed class to set up a heaven on earth is more important to us than a unity in proletarian opinion about the imaginary paradise in the sky' (p. 10).

Nevertheless atheistic education does have a place in the Communist attack on religion, although it is subordinate to the proletarian revolution. This is consistent with Communist convictions concerning the factors at work in human life: economic factors are decisive, but the superstructure of ideas may also react to influence processes of social change. Moreover, Communism since the 1917 Revolution in Russia has stressed the importance of *conscious understanding and acceptance* of Marxism-Leninism if men are to bring in socialism and communism without undue delay; 'spontaneous' political activity which merely happens to promote the Communist cause is not enough. Since religious belief can be a serious obstacle to a conscious understanding and acceptance of Marxism-Leninism, it should be undermined as much as possible—even though economic changes have not yet made its disappearance inevitable. Hence Communist governments should restrain religious propaganda and promote anti-religious propaganda.

The fundamental Communist conviction, however, is that history is on the side of atheism. Religion will die a 'natural death' as men gain control over their relations of production under socialism and then under communism. Hence both Marx and Lenin insisted that there is no need for Communists to foster religious fanaticism by direct persecution of believers. Of course, where religious believers act or think in counter-revolutionary ways they must be dealt with in the same way as other class enemies.

(In practice, there have been severe religious persecutions in Communist countries.)

What does the Christian Believe about Nature, Man and God?

The material world matters

Christian faith is faith in God as Creator, Saviour and King. Where this faith is rightly understood, it is positive in its attitude to the material world. Christianity is 'the most avowedly materialistic of all the great religions' (William Temple).

Christians believe in God as the Creator of all things. He is the Creator not only of man's mental and spiritual powers but also of human bodies and the whole physical universe. In God's eye, the material world is good, real and important, and man is a psycho-physical unity, whose 'religious' life must not be separated from his 'secular' life. Christian faith affirms the reality of *this* world: the world of molecules and men, of genes and machines, of stars and super-states. Since this world matters to God, it should not be despised or ignored by man.

Christians believe in God as the Saviour of all men. 'The Word was made flesh and dwelt among us.' The Son of God came into the world, identifying himself with humanity, and hallowing the bread and wine for which man toils. He came with the gift of eternal life, which is a new quality of life *on earth.* (This new life will be continued and fulfilled in heaven, but it begins in the here and now.) He revealed the divine concern for man's material needs: food and shelter, health and friendship. He called men to share in this concern. He gave men the power, not to escape from society, but to serve it. This power he continues to give.

Christians believe in God as King of all the future. Christians pray, 'Thy Kingdom come, Thy will be done on earth as it is in heaven'. Christians live in hope for a 'new heaven and a new earth' and a 'resurrection of the body'. That is, they believe that, in the end, God will transform nature and humanity. The transformation is a mystery, but one thing is clear: the new world will have an essential connection with this world. So even the 'other-worldly' hope of Christians involves a hope for this world, for the new world will be a fulfilment of the old.

Man is God's steward over nature

The Christian faith, rightly understood, is compatible with modern man's attempt to explain and control the processes of nature. Indeed, modern science arose in Western culture rather than elsewhere because the religious presuppositions of Christians (and also of Jews and Muslims) provided a basis for a scientific attitude towards nature.

Christians believe that man is God's appointed steward over nature, God's representative to whom he has delegated authority. Man must recognize that his stewardship is not an absolute ownership, that his authority over nature is subject to God's authority over him. These limitations should be acknowledged. Nevertheless God's purpose is that man should gain more and more control over his natural environment. God is not like the 'god' of the Promethean myth who was jealous of human power over nature. If man discovers fire or atomic secrets, he is not 'stealing' them from God. However, if man rejects his authority, these secrets bring evil rather than good to the world.

Since nature is God's creation, nature is not divine and nature is not a 'part' of God—as some men have believed. So men are not being impious or irreverent when they pry out the secrets of nature by ingenious experiments. Moreover, the regularities of nature are for Christians a sign of God's reliability and faithfulness to man. The scientist's assumption that nature is orderly is undergirded by a Christian faith that God is dependable.

Sin is the root of moral evil

Christians believe that all men are sinners. This does not merely mean that all men do evil, though this is true. More fundamentally, all men are alienated from God. Men reject their dependence on him as Creator, deny their need for him as Saviour, and shape their own futures in rebellion against him as King. Sin is this alienation or estrangement from God; it is the basic cause of man's alienation from man. Sin cannot be overcome by human effort, but only by God, who evokes in men a response of faith: a response of humility, trust and obedience. In Christ, God has reconciled men to himself and to one another. This reconciliation is proclaimed in the Gospel. It is implemented by men insofar as they respond to what God has done, inspired by his Holy Spirit.

Sin is not only an individual matter. It involves society, for a man's personality consists partly of his relations with other men. This means that the alienation of men from God consists not only in their internal states as individuals; it also includes their external relations within the structures of human society. Man's rebellion against God is expressed not only in inner attitudes such as pride and malice, not only in specific crimes such as theft and murder, but also in social injustices for which no one person is responsible, although all men are implicated: unemployment, exploitation, racial discrimination and political oppression. God's purpose for men is to transform both individuals and social structures. He works to overcome both the alienation within men and the alienation between men.

Is sin the *only* cause of moral evil in individuals and societies?
Is the Gospel the *only* remedy for moral evil?
No.

Sin is the decisive cause and the Gospel is the decisive remedy; but there are secondary causes for which secondary remedies are needed. The Gospel is not an exclusive panacea which prohibits all attempts to improve individuals and societies by secular means. It would be folly to deny that some men may become better men because of moral instruction or vocational guidance or psychoanalysis or simple friendliness. Moreover, it is clear that a society may become a better society because of legislation against discrimination, public works for the unemployed, or amnesty to political prisoners. But it is folly to hope for an elimination of human egoism and greed for power if one is relying solely on human planning and human willing; for the fundamental flaw remains untouched. Men are alienated from God, and must respond to him if they are to be reconciled with him.

Sin is man's attempt to raise himself to the level of God. Man is free to form his own image of himself, and since the possibilities seem to be unlimited, he has delusions of divine grandeur. He imagines that he could and should be infinite in power and knowledge and goodness and importance. Man is actually limited in power and knowledge and goodness and importance, but he refuses to recognize this. He tries to hide these limits from himself by seeking unlimited power over others, by claiming to know the final truth, by asserting himself self-righteously in his deeds, and by concocting ideologies: systems of religion or philosophy which help him to feel important and meaningful *apart from God.* All men do this, whether they be religious or irreligious. Indeed, religious men are specially prone to these forms of self-idolatry and self-deception. Christians are no exception. But Christians should be able to recognize and acknowledge the self-interest which infects their own claims to power, truth, goodness and importance. A Christian is in a position to accept the humiliating judgment of God upon his proud and hypocritical pretensions because this judgment comes to him along with an assurance of divine forgiveness and a call to share in the divine life. In Christ, God has *given* to all men the divine dignity which as sinners they try to *grasp*: in Christ they can become the sons of God. Sin is failure to love the God who loves man.

Sin is also the failure to love the man whom God loves. In Jesus' account of the Last Judgment (Matt. 25.31-46), the sinners whom he rejects are those who have been callous and careless in relation to the physical and personal needs of their fellow men. All men are in danger of committing this sin: believers and unbelievers, Christians and atheists. The sin of selfishness is neither seemly nor subtle, but all men are prone to it. Christians who misunderstand the doctrine of justification by faith may even reinforce such sin by thinking of faith as a *substitute* for the good works of love and justice which God requires. But genuine Christian faith is a grateful acceptance of God's indwelling power, which inspires and enables man to love his neighbour as himself.

God overcomes sin in men if they acknowledge their *own* sin. 'A Christian should begin with his own sin, with the beam in his own eye, and not with the sins of his neighbours or of those who belong to another group or who are on the other side of some conflict . . . This is difficult enough for a Christian in his personal relations but it is vastly more difficult for the Christian as a citizen or as a member of an economic or political group. In political life we tend to be guided by black and white slogans, by ideological prejudice, by self-righteous patriotism or party spirit and yet, in spite of the difficulty in this sphere, the habit of beginning with the sin of one's nation, with the sin of one's own "side", should be natural within the Christian community' (John C. Bennett, *Christians and the State*, p. 56).

Men are called to a blessed fellowship with God

Christians believe that blessedness or supreme happiness consists in a life of fellowship with God. During his earthly life, the Christian has some experience of the inner peace and joy which God's presence brings. He believes that this is a hint of the joys of heaven, a glimpse of the limitless happiness which God has prepared for those who love him. The reward which is promised to Christians is the goal of the Christian pilgrimage on earth, for the reward is God himself.

The sublime Christian hope does not conflict with this-worldly emphasis of the Christian faith. The God whose presence brings joy is the God who is to be found in costly service of his children and in thankful appreciation of his creatures. An other-worldly faith which tries to bypass the Cross and the physical world is pseudo-Christian. Christians join hands with unbelievers in this-worldly service to their fellow men.

Nevertheless, Christian service has an additional motive. For a Christian the supreme goal in life is that men should come to know God. So a Christian who shares an unbeliever's concern for the material and psychological needs of men, will have an additional concern. His supreme motive in life is to be a person whom God can use to reveal himself to men. His actions should help to convey the reality and presence of God. For example, if he helps a man in trouble, the Christian wants the man to feel not only that 'somebody cares', but also (and *because of this*) that 'God cares'. The service of another man must aim to meet not only his material needs, but also his deepest need: his need for fellowship with God. The life and actions of a Christian man and a Christian community should move others to glorify God. 'Let your light so shine before men that they may see your good works and glorify your Father which is in heaven' (Matt. 5.16).

Since each individual man is called to a life of fellowship with God, he has dignity, worth and importance in the eyes of God. He is a brother for whom Christ died, a potential son of God. In the Gospels, we meet many a man who was a brother for whom Christ *lived* as well as died; Jesus revealed God's love for all sorts and conditions of men. No man should be deprived of his fundamental human rights merely because of the group to which he belongs—his race, religion, or class. No man should be used merely as a means to an end. Moreover, Christians should not assume that a man is beyond the reach of the Gospel merely because of his professed atheism. As Johannes Hamel has said concerning some of the Communists who persecute him: 'This so completely religionless man among us has a fine ear for the voice of the Living God . . . These estranged fanatics, who seem to be in another world, are really very close to faith . . . Even today the divine sword continues tirelessly to smash the ideological armour in which these people live. If only all Christians would take it in their hands!' (*A Christian in East Germany*, p. 33).

God reveals himself to the eyes of faith

God's existence cannot be proved or disproved. The astronaut, the experimenter and the logician are in no better position than anyone else in deciding whether God exists. God reveals himself in various ways to *all* men, but not as the solution to a problem. God comes as a mystery to whom men respond in faith—that is, in awe and trust and obedience. He has revealed himself uniquely in the life and death and resurrection of Jesus, and he continues to reveal himself through the risen Jesus to the Church.

God is like man, for he created man in his own image. Man, however, tends to create ideas of 'God' in his own image, and since man's image of himself is distorted by sin, his idea of

God is also distorted. This often leads to idolatry: the conscious or unconscious worship of man rather than God. So, although God confirms whatever is good and true in man's religion, he rejects the pride and false ideology in man's religion. Only Jesus Christ is the true man, man in the image of God, man in perfect relation to God. All others 'come short of the glory of God'. In Jesus, God not only revealed himself; he also revealed what it means to be a *man*.

The revelation of God and man in Jesus Christ is neither proved nor disproved by science. It is either accepted in faith or rejected in unfaith.

Commentary

Disagreements with Communism

(1) Christians must reject the *theoretical atheism* of Communism. Indeed, it seems obvious that Communists have not disproved the existence of God at all.

Consider, first of all, the Communist explanations of the origins of religious beliefs. Even if these explanations were completely adequate (which they are not), this would not prove that religious beliefs are false. An explanation of the psychological origins of a belief does not in itself show anything concerning the truth or falsity of the belief. This is so in the case of *dis*belief as well: a psychological explanation of the origins of an atheist's disbelief does not prove that he is mistaken either. The psychological origin of a belief is one thing; its truth or falsity is another.

The five Communist arguments for atheism which were outlined are also faulty:

1. A Christian may agree with the Communist claim that the existence of God cannot be proved by observation, science or logic; for this does not show that the existence of God can be *dis*proved by observation, science or logic.

2. The Communist merely assumes that the world has always existed. He cannot prove this as yet, since it is still a matter for scientific and philosophical investigation. More-

over, even if someone did prove that the world did not have a beginning, this would not disprove the existence of the Creator. The fundamental Christian belief concerning the Creator is that everything depends on him for its existence at *any* time. If the world has always existed, then it has always depended on God the Creator for its existence. He could annihilate it at any time, merely by ceasing to sustain it in existence.

3. The Communist merely assumes that his dogma, 'Whatever is immaterial depends on the material' applies to God. Even if a Christian agreed that it applies to everything except God, he would not need to agree that it applies to God.

4. A Christian need not deny that human labour has been immensely important in the development of man throughout history. But how can a Communist prove that God was *not* at work in human history, revealing to men what it means to be a man rather than a beast?

5. Communist scepticism concerning whether Jesus ever existed is completely unfounded. This scepticism (which is not universal among Communists) arose from Engels and Lenin, who depended on speculative theories rather than serious historical scholarship. (See Hans-Gerhard Koch, *The Abolition of God.*)

All these replies show that the dogmatic atheism of Communists depends on assumptions which can be challenged. Communists would be much wiser if they were agnostic rather than atheist. The agnostic says, 'I do not know whether God exists or not', whereas the atheist says, 'I know that God does not exist'.

Communists evade the central Christian claim, which concerns Jesus of Nazareth. As Alexander Miller said, 'Christianity rests upon the historic fact of Christ, upon the prophetic witness which testified to him and upon the apostolic witness in which the meaning of his coming is set forth. The question, then, is whether Christian doctrine gives a valid and true interpretation of these facts. Marxism generally does not deal with them at all' (*The Christian Significance of Karl Marx,* pp. 90-1).

Alasdair MacIntyre made a similar point: 'The issue that is really evaded by Marxism here is that of the historical Jesus. Marx condemns religion as Idealist. But religion is only idealist if its myth is a substitute for history. The gospel claims that in the person of Jesus myth became history, the ideal became real' (*Marxism, An Interpretation,* p. 87).

(2) Christians must also reject the *practical atheism* of Communism. When Lenin cries, 'Down with God! Long live nature!', this is not a theoretical disproof of God's existence; it is a vehement rejection of a God who may very well exist. The attitude of proud defiance arises from a wilful self-deception, a refusal to recognize the limits of man, a rejection of God's righteous judgment on human pretensions. Communists have a faith in Communist man which leads them to claim absolute righteousness for their cause. (Christians sometimes make similar self-righteous claims, but this is done in spite of their Christian faith, not because of it.)

Communist faith in man could be shared by many Christians if it were merely an insistence on the dignity and worth and possibilities of mankind. Communists, however, insist on making this faith in man an absolute faith so that man is set in the place of God. Communism becomes a religion. Religious rites and worshipful language are adopted for Communist use in services of dedication to Communism and hymns in praise of Communist leaders. The result is sometimes a ludicrous and blasphemous parody of the Christian faith.

Communist governments vary in their tactics concerning the extent to which they will permit a partial acceptance of Communist ideology. There is a general tendency, however, to assert the totalitarian claims of Communism, and to demand an atheistic faith in man and an unlimited loyalty to the party and the state. Christians must reject this demand.

(3) Christians must reject Communist *totalitarianism* insofar as it 'writes off' individuals who do not belong to the proletariat or identify themselves with the interests of the proletariat as interpreted by the Party. In the eyes of God, all men have rights and worth. The interests of individuals must not

be completely subordinated to those of the group. (We shall consider this further in Chapter IV.)

Agreements with Communism

(1) Christians should agree with Communists in insisting on the importance of *this* world, and the *material* needs of men. Too often in the past Christians have been guilty of another form of 'practical atheism': unlike the Communists they have worshipped God, but they have neglected the hungry, the homeless and the helpless. They have said 'Lord, Lord', but they have not done the will of God. In a world of suffering and exploitation, the 'this-worldly' moral zeal of some atheistic Communists is probably more acceptable to God than the 'other-worldly' indifference of some Christians.

(2) Christians should also accept the Communist's enthusiasm for science, which, of course, is not confined to Communists. God has appointed man to control nature for human welfare. (Christians must acknowledge however, that man's authority over nature is an authority *under* God.)

(3) Christians should also admit to Communists (and to God, who is our supreme critic) that there is a great deal of truth in Communist criticisms of religion—not only other religions, but the Christian religion. In each case, however, the criticism has force because the Christian faith has not been rightly understood or genuinely practised. Moreover, there are criticisms of Communist faith which need to be made in all honesty. Let us consider the Communist criticisms in turn:

(i) Religion as *unrealistic idealism*. Christians must admit that the Church has often made an unrealistic appeal to human idealism instead of dealing realistically with injustices on the level of economic and political power. For example, some Christians pleaded with nineteenth-century capitalists to be kind, but opposed the organization of trade unions.

But the Christian faith, rightly understood, is a faith in *God*, not a faith in the 'power of ideas'. On the other hand, Christian faith is not a faith in the power of economic forces either. Christians are free to grant varying degrees of importance to *ideas* on the one and *economics* on the other hand.

Moreover, Christians must insist that Communists are unrealistic concerning human nature. Since Communists hold that the ultimate source of evil lies in the economic power structure of society, they are unready and unable to deal with evils which arise in their 'socialistic' society—for example, abuses of police power. They ignore Acton's proverb: 'Power tends to corrupt, and absolute power corrupts absolutely.'

(ii) Religion as man's *creative fantasy*. Christians must admit that man often creates 'God' in his own image. All religious men, including Christians, are in grave danger of doing this. Indeed, it is part of the explanation not only of gross idolatry but also of the fact that Christians differ in their ideas of God. Also, it is true that some Christians have mistakenly thought that the best way to glorify God is to denigrate man, cheating man of all dignity and worth.

But Christian faith, rightly understood, insists on the dignity and worth of man. The Christian faith is faith in a revelation of God concerning both God and man. In Jesus, Christians recognize not only true God but also true man.

It is not folly but wisdom to create one's ideas of God in the image of Jesus; for thus one comes to know God as he really is. In the life of Jesus we see the possibilities of man, and by the power of the risen Christ we are enabled to realize these possibilities. When Marx says, 'The more a man relies on God, the less of himself he retains', he is mistaken.

(iii) Religion as *illusion* and *ideology*. Christians must admit that the Christian religion and other religions have often been opiates which the ruling classes used to keep the masses submissive. Christians must also admit that their own convictions, like those of all men, are always in danger of becoming distorted into mere ideology. ('Ideology', we remember, was originally Marx's term for a self-deceiving system of ideas which sounds very noble but which is really a 'cover' for one's own economic self-interest. Communists claim, however, that one ideology is true: Marxism-Leninism.)

But Christian faith cannot agree that it provides only an 'illusory' happiness. Man has deep spiritual needs which remain unsatisfied without God, and which *are* satisfied by

God. The joys and hopes of believers in the presence of God are not 'illusory'. Moreover, the Christian faith, rightly understood, is not an ideology. Indeed, it contains its own corrective to ideology (though the corrective is obviously not always applied). The Christian's understanding of sin and his assurance of divine forgiveness and divine destiny help him to face up to the disguised self-interest in his own thinking.

Moreover, Christians will point out that the Communist's notion of ideology is inadequate. Men do not merely concoct ideas to protect their own *economic* self-interest. They are also interested in justifying their claims to power, asserting their righteousness over other men, and establishing their importance in the universe. Much Communist thinking is 'ideological' in this more profound sense of the word, and Communist faith reinforces the self-deception.

(iv) Religion as *pseudo-science*. Christians must admit that the Christian and other religions have often included a great deal of superstitious credulity and ignorant fear, and that this is gradually disappearing as science progresses, explaining more and more about nature and society.

But Christian faith, rightly understood, is not a faith in a 'God of the gaps' in science. Christian faith does not depend on unscientific inferences to 'God' wherever there is something in nature which scientists cannot as yet explain or control. Communist attacks on the 'God of the gaps' are attacks on something which contemporary Christian theology also rejects.

Moreover, Christians must insist that a scientific explanation of events does not eliminate mystery or revelation, and that scientific method is not the only way by which man comes to know truth.

Christian Options

Christians are *free* to accept much or little of Communist 'historical materialism' insofar as it explains the processes of human history in terms of the economic structures of society. The Communist account includes factual claims which are open to the investigations of historians and social scientists. Christian faith does not dictate the conclusions for these investigations. For example, the Christian faith does not tell us whether the main factors producing parliamentary democracy in seventeenth-century England were religious or economic. As Alexander Miller rightly says, 'What the Christian Gospel affirms is not the primacy of the spiritual over the material, or the power of ideas in history, but the rule of God over all'.

Christians who agree concerning the rule of God over all nevertheless may differ concerning the relative importance of materialistic and idealistic factors in history.

On the one hand, there is Christian Marxism. As Marxism, it is the historical conviction that economic factors are primary and that economic and political changes in society are more effective than the idealism of individuals. As *Christian* Marxism, it is the theological conviction that these changes are vehicles of God's action in history. Alexander Miller has said this:

'It is not part of the Christian thesis that ideals have been more powerful in history than brute facts: as if God were able to manipulate ideas, but a bit helpless when it came to the sphere of the material and economic . . . The Christian's only interest is in getting at the truth of the matter. If he has taken his Bible seriously, he will not be taken aback in the least to find that economic interest conditions very largely the ideas men hold, and determines very largely the action that they take as individuals and as groups. We ought therefore if the evidence warrants—as I am very sure that it does—to be ready to accept Marxism as giving us the essence of a scientific sociology' (*The Christian Significance of Karl Marx*, pp. 88-9).

Miller later expressed reservations concerning Marxism as 'the essence of a scientific sociology'. Some Christians would agree with his original claim, while others would reject it. In neither case is the issue settled by an appeal to Christian faith. Critics of Marxism have *other* reasons for rejecting its claim to provide the scientific account of history. Karl Popper, for example, says that 'although the *general* importance of Marx's economism (materialism) can hardly be overrated, it is very easy to overrate the importance of the economic conditions in any *particular* case'. He warns us not to take Marxism too seriously: 'We must regard it as nothing more than a most valuable suggestion to us to consider things in their relation to their economic background' (*The Open Society and its Enemies,* Vol. II, London, 1962, pp. 107, 110).

Christians differ in the degree to which they accept a Marxist emphasis on economic factors in history. But even those who accept Marxism as a 'scientific sociology' are not necessarily pro-Communist. Communism is not merely a broadly Marxist interpretation of man and history. Communism is a particular political movement led by a specific group, the Communist Party, which demands unqualified allegiance and which claims absolute authority in the interpretation and application of Marxism.

In sharp contrast with Christian Marxists there are Christian 'idealists' who hold that changes in history come from transformed individuals, so that the removal of injustice in society depends primarily on changes in individuals. This historical conviction may be combined with a theological conviction that God works primarily through individuals or small groups rather than economic power-structures. Emil Brunner has said, 'The primary function of the Church is not to change structures, that is, legal and organized systems, but to change the intention by the vital union of individuals and the community with the living and present Lord Jesus. Where there are people permeated with the Spirit of Christ, right relationships, laws and arrangements always follow' (*Communism, Capitalism and Christianity,* p. 43).

Christians will generally agree that Brunner has set forth the primary function of the Church for most situations. But many will question his claim that problems of power-structure are automatically resolved by people who are 'permeated with the Spirit of Christ'. No Christian community in history has completely resolved these problems within itself, let alone for the rest of mankind. The Gospel is not a panacea.

In The United Church of Canada Christians differ in their emphases, but there is a general concern to stress *both* the idealistic and materialistic factors in human life and in the tasks of the Church.

3

Property and Economics

What does the Communist Believe about Property and Economics?

In the previous chapters we have already had a glimpse of Communist economics, for the Marxist-Leninist doctrine of man is fundamentally a matter of economics. However, we did not study the core of Communist economics, which claims to be an account of processes which lead inevitably from capitalism through socialism to communism.

We shall now consider this in four sections. The first section is an outline of a basic Marxist concept in economics: 'exploitation'. In the other sections we shall quote from the *New Programme of the Communist Party of the Soviet Union* (1961). Section two summarizes the teachings of Marx and Lenin concerning capitalism. Section three is a sketch of Marxist-Leninist 'socialism'. Section four deals with the transition from socialism to communism.

We shall state the Communist convictions without comment or criticism. This procedure does not mean that we endorse all these convictions. Many of them are open to powerful objections from non-Communist economists, and some of them involve value-judgments which Christians should reject (as we shall see in the Commentary). But if Christians are to understand what Communists actually believe, they must study Communist convictions, not non-Communist interpretations of these convictions.

Exploitation

The fundamental idea in Marxist economics is that the

capitalist class exploits the proletariat. Capitalists profit because of the 'surplus-value' which the proletariat produces.

The value of any commodity is the amount of labour-power spent on its production.

Labour itself is a commodity, which the capitalist buys for its value.

The value of a labourer, the cost of using a labourer for a day, is merely the amount required to produce and support a labourer at a subsistence level for a day.

The labourer works for, say, six hours to produce the equivalent of this labour-value. This is the 'necessary labour-time'.

If the employer uses the labourer for ten hours a day, the additional four hours are surplus labour-time, the commodities produced during this extra period are surplus-products, and their value is surplus-value.

Thus the worker provides more labour than is needed to produce his wages. The capitalist *exploits* him.

The capitalist has the economic power to exploit him because he owns the means of production.

Exploitation is inevitable under a capitalist system. The only remedy is the abolition of capitalism, and its replacement by socialism. Private ownership of the means of production must be replaced by public ownership.

It is important to distinguish between two kinds of property:

(a) Social property (producer's goods)—the means of production, such as land, tools, and factories.

(b) Personal property (consumer's goods)—food, clothes, houses, cars, etc.

Communists advocate public ownership of producer's goods, but they do not advocate the abolition of all private property. Consumer's goods can remain in the private possession of individuals.

Exploitation is inevitable under a capitalist system. Moral denunciation of individual capitalists is natural, but it is ineffective and inappropriate, for the surplus-value wage system is the only feasible system under capitalism.

Communists strive, not for a larger labour slice of the productive pie, but for a non-exploiting socialist system which will produce a bigger pie, that is, an abundance of consumer's goods for individuals.

Communists are convinced that capitalist exploitation generates various contradictions which lead inevitably to the collapse of capitalism and its overthrow in a proletarian revolution. This establishes socialism, which leads on to communism. Thus, according to the *New Programme of the Communist Party of the Soviet Union*, 'Marxism-Leninism discovered the objective laws of social development and revealed the contradictions inherent in capitalism, the inevitability of their bringing about a revolutionary explosion and of the transition of society to communism'.

The New Programme provides an excellent summary of Communist convictions concerning capitalism, socialism and communism. Anyone who is not familiar with Marxism-Leninism will find the language of the New Programme difficult, but it is worth the effort. (Quotations are from *Essential Works of Marxism,* ed. A. P. Mendel; all italics are ours.)

The Communist view of Capitalism

Exploitation

According to the New Programme, 'Capitalism is the last exploiting system. Having developed its productive forces to an enormous extent, it became a tremendous obstacle to social progress . . . The growing conflict between productive *forces* and productive *relations* imperatively demands that mankind should break the decayed capitalist shell, release the powerful productive forces created by man and use them for the good of society as a whole.'

'Whatever the specific character of the rise and development of capitalism in any country, that system has everywhere common features and objective laws.'

'Under capitalism, the basic and decisive means of production belong to the numerically small capitalistic class, while the vast majority of the population consists of proletarians and semi-proletarians, who own no means of production and are therefore compelled to sell their labour-power and by their labour create profits and riches for the ruling classes of society. The bourgeois state, *whatever its form*, is an instrument of the domination of labour by capital.'

'The development of large-scale capitalist production—production for profit, for the appropriation of surplus value—leads to the elimination of small independent producers, makes them wholly dependent on capital. Capitalism extensively exploits female and child labour. The economic laws of its development necessarily give rise to a huge reserve army of unemployed, which is constantly replenished by ruined peasants and urban petty bourgeoisie. The exploitation of the working people is continuously increasing, social inequality is becoming more and more marked, the gulf between the haves and the have-nots is widening, and the sufferings and privations of the millions are growing worse.'

Contradictions

According to the New Programme, 'Capitalism, by concentrating millions of workers in its factories, socializing the process of labour, imparts a social character to production; nevertheless it is the capitalists who appropriate the fruits of labour. This fundamental contradiction of capitalism—the contradiction between the *social character of production* and the *private-capitalist form of appropriation*—manifests itself in *productive anarchy* and in the fact that the *purchasing power of society falls short* of the expansion of production and leads periodically to destructive economic *crises*. Crises and periods of industrial stagnation, in turn, are still more ruinous to small producers, increase the dependence of wage-labour on capital and lead more rapidly to a relative and sometimes an absolute deterioration of the condition of the working class.'

Imperialism

The New Programme goes on to describe the final stage of capitalism, which it calls 'imperialism':

'The process of concentration and centralization of capital, while destroying free competition, led in the early twentieth century to the establishment of powerful capitalist monopoly associations—syndicates, cartels and trusts—which acquired decisive importance in the economy, to the merging of bank capital and immensely concentrated industrial capital, and to intensive export of capital . . . Capitalism has entered its final stage, the stage of monopoly capitalism, of *imperialism.*'

'The imperialist powers' struggle for markets, for spheres of capital investment, for raw materials and labour, and for world domination became more intense than ever. In an epoch of the undivided rule of imperialism, that struggle necessarily led to devastating wars.'

'Imperialism is decaying and moribund capitalism, it is the eve of the Socialist revolution. The world capitalist system as a whole is ripe for the social revolution of the proletariat.'

Final crisis

The New Programme gives a long list of alleged facts which Communists cite as signs of final crisis:

'The breakaway from capitalism of more and more countries; the weakening of imperialist positions in the economic competition with socialism; the break-up of the imperialist colonial system; the intensification of imperialist contradictions with the development of state-monopoly capitalism and the growth of militarism; the mounting internal instability and decay of capitalist economy evidenced by the increasing inability of capitalism to make full use of the productive forces (low rates of production growth, periodic crises, continuous underloading of production plant, and chronic unemployment); the mounting struggle between labour and capital; an acute intensification of contradictions within the world capitalist economy; and unprecedented growth of political reaction in all spheres, rejection of bourgeois freedoms and establishment of Fascist and despotic regimes in a number of countries, and the profound crisis of bourgeois policy and ideology—all these are manifestations of the general crisis of capitalism.'

Objections rejected

The New Programme rejects the objections of non-Communists who claim that capitalism has improved:

'Fear of revolution, the successes of the Socialist countries and the pressure of the working-class movement compel the bourgeoisie to make partial concessions with respect to wages, labour conditions and social security. But more often than not mounting prices and inflation reduce these concessions to naught. Wages lag behind the daily material and cultural requirements of the worker and his family, which grow as society develops.'

'Even the relatively high standard of living in the small group of capitalistically developed countries rests upon the poverty of the Asian, African and Latin-American peoples, upon non-equivalent exchange, discrimination of female labour, brutal oppression of Negroes and immigrant workers, and also upon the intensified exploitation of the working people in those countries.'[1]

'Life has fully confirmed the Marxist thesis of increasing proletarization in capitalist society. The expropriated masses have no other prospect of acquiring property than the revolutionary establishment of the social ownership of means of production, that is, making them the property of the whole people.'

The Communist view of Socialism

The New Programme goes on to say a great deal about socialism, which began in Russia with the 1917 Revolution. Four main claims should be noted:

(i) Socialism has eliminated two basic defects of capitalism.

[1] Chinese Communist ideology goes beyond the Russian New Programme at this point. The Russians still emphasize the class struggle between bourgeois and proletarian classes *within capitalist countries.* The Chinese, however, see the class struggle much more as a struggle *between* countries: major capitalist countries versus the underprivileged (but largely non-proletarian) masses in Asia, Africa and Latin America. (D.E.)

(ii) Socialism retains two features of capitalism, though in modified form.

(iii) Socialism requires a Marxist-Leninist people.

(iv) Socialism assumes that the Party must have a dominant role in society, even during the period of 'Communist construction' which leads to communism.

Socialism and the defects of capitalism

The New Programme claims that public ownership of the means of production has eliminated the two fundamental defects of the capitalist economic system: exploitation of labour and inhibition of production.

Labour *exploitation* has disappeared because the people as a whole[2] own the means of production. The working class are aware that 'they work for themselves and their society and not for exploiters'. This freedom from exploitation is thought to be the 'highest manifestation' of individual liberty; it is 'what primarily constitutes genuine social justice'.

Concerning *production*, the Programme claims that 'all in all, capitalism is increasingly impeding the development of the contemporary productive forces. Mankind is entering the period of great scientific and technical revolution . . . but the relations of production under capitalism are much too narrow for a scientific and technical revolution.' In contrast with this, 'socialism has created conditions for the rapid progress of science. The achievements of Soviet science clearly show the superiority of the Socialist system. . . . It is only logical that the country of victorious socialism should have ushered in the era of the utilization of atomic energy for peaceful purposes, and that it should have blazed a trail into outer space.'

[2] The Yugoslav Communist Party differs from the Russian Party (and even more from the Chinese Party) concerning public ownership. Although much of the economy is to be owned by the government (the people as a whole) and all of it is to be co-ordinated by the government, the Yugoslav Party gives not only tactical concessions but also strong theoretical support to co-operative ownership of means of production by smaller groups.

Socialism and similarities to capitalism

Although the exploitation of labour and the inhibition of production have been eliminated, Socialism does retain two features of capitalism: Income is not yet distributed according to individual need, and there is a coercive state which promotes the interests of a ruling class. In each case, however, the capitalist feature is radically modified.

Incomes vary greatly under socialism. According to the New Programme, 'The Socialist principle "From each according to his abilities, *to each according to his work*" has been put into effect in the Soviet Union.[3] This principle insures that the members of society have a material interest in the fruits of labour; it makes it possible to harmonize personal and social interests in the most effective way and serves as a powerful stimulus for increasing productivity of labour, developing the economy and raising the people's standards of living.' But although Socialism does not apply the Communist principle 'to each according to his *need*', it differs from capitalism in that everyone *must* work for a living and everyone *can* work for a living; neither capitalist drones nor labour unemployed exist.

Socialism involves a coercive state, the 'dictatorship of the proletariat'. This replaces the 'dictatorship of the bourgeoisie'. 'A bourgeois republic, however democratic, however hallowed by slogans purporting to express the will of the people or nation as a whole, or an extra-class will, inevitably remains in practice—owing to the existence of private capitalist ownership of the means of production—a dictatorship of the bourgeoisie, a machine for the exploitation and suppression of the vast majority of the working people by a handful of capitalists. In contrast to the bourgeoisie, which conceals the class character of the state, the working class does not deny the class character of states. The dictatorship of the proletariat is

[3] The Chinese Communist Party differs from the Russian Party in that it minimizes the need for such material incentives during socialism. (D.E.)

a dictatorship of the overwhelming majority over the minority.'[4]

According to the New Programme, it is necessary for the proletariat to overthrow the bourgeois state, replacing it by a proletarian state. In this revolution, violence is usually (though not always) necessary, since the ruling class rarely yield their power without a fight.[5] The new state must also continue to wield coercive power so as to meet two threats: the threat of internal counter-revolution and the threat of external attack by capitalist countries. Another reason given for the powerful state apparatus in the Soviet Union is the need for strong central government during the enforced industrialization of the country. Although socialist revolutions often occur in pre-industrial countries, 'by-passing the capitalist stage of development', the industrialization itself cannot be by-passed if communism is eventually to be achieved.

Socialism and a Marxist-Leninist people

'Under socialism . . . the shaping of a scientific world outlook in all working people is of prime importance. The ideological basis of this world outlook is shaped as Marxism-Leninism, an integral and harmonious system of philosophical, economic and socio-political views. The party calls for the education of the population as a whole in the spirit of scientific communism and strives to insure that all working people master the ideas of Marxism-Leninism, that they fully under-

[4] The Russian and Chinese Parties differ concerning how long this dictatorship must last. The New Programme depicts Russia as having already moved beyond the dictatorship of the proletariat to enter a 'democracy of the people as a whole', a period of 'Communist construction'. The Chinese hold that 'five or ten generations' of proletarian dictatorship will be necessary in order to protect the revolution against counterrevolutionary or 'capitalistic' tendencies; they claim, indeed, that such tendencies have already subverted Russian socialism, which is no longer on the true path to communism. (D.E.)

[5] The Chinese Communist Party differs from the Russian Party (and even more from the Italian Party) in that it minimizes the likelihood of peaceful progress towards socialism by means of 'structural reforms' within capitalism, or a non-violent proletarian revolution.

stand the course and perspectives of world development, take a correct view of international and domestic events and consciously build their life on Communist lines. Communist ideas and Communist deeds should blend organically in the behaviour of every person and in the activities of all collectives and organizations' (New Programme).

Socialism and Party leadership

'Unlike all the preceding socio-economic formations, Communist society does not develop sporadically, but as a result of conscious and purposeful efforts of the masses led by the Marxist-Leninist party. The Communist party, which unites the foremost representatives of the working people and is closely connected with the masses, which enjoys *unbounded authority* among the people and understands the laws of social development, provides proper leadership in Communist construction as a whole, giving it an organized, planned and scientifically based character' (New Programme).

In the Conclusion of the official *Short History of the Communist Party of the Soviet Union* the following claim is made concerning Marxist doctrine: 'It enables the Party to find the right orientation in any situation, to understand the inner connection of current events, to foresee their course, and to perceive not only how and in what direction they are developing in the present, but how and in what direction they are bound to develop in the future.'[6]

Communism

Part II of the New Programme begins with a clear summary of their convictions concerning communism:

'What is communism?'

'Communism is *a classless social system* with one form of

[6] Some Communists now have reservations concerning such a claim, which makes the Party virtually infallible. For example, Adam Schaff in Poland holds that an individual sometimes should follow his own judgment rather than submit to party discipline if he is convinced that a Party action is harmful to the Communist cause. (D.E.)

public ownership of the means of production and full social equality of all members of society; under it, *the all-round development of people* will be accompanied by the growth of the productive forces through continuous progress in science and technology, *all sources of public wealth will gush forth abundantly*, and the great principle "From each according to his ability, *to each according to his needs*" will be implemented. Communism is a highly organized society of free, socially conscious people in which *public self-government* will be established, in which labour for the good of society will become the prime and vital requirement of everyone, a *necessity recognized by one and all.*'

Each of the words or phrases which we have italicized indicates an important element in communism which the New Programme attempts to explain:

A classless social system:

'Communism puts an end to the division of society into classes and social strata, whereas the whole history of mankind, with the exception of its primitive period, was one of class society in which division into opposing classes led to the exploitation of man by man, class struggle, and antagonisms between nations and states.'

(Even under socialism a class struggle has existed, between the proletariat ruling class and the remnants of earlier ruling classes. 'The class struggle does not disappear in the period of the building of socialism.')

The all-round development of people:

'In the period of transition to communism, there are greater opportunities of educating a new man, who will harmoniously combine spiritual wealth, moral purity and a perfect physique.

'As less and less time is spent on material production, the individual is afforded ever greater opportunities to develop his abilities, gifts and talents in the fields of production, science, engineering, literature and the arts.'

'Communism is the system under which the abilities and talents of free man, his best moral qualities, blossom forth and reveal themselves in full. Family relations will be completely freed from material considerations and will be based solely on mutual love and friendship.'

An abundance of consumer's goods:

'Communism insures the continuous development of social production and high labour productivity through rapid scientific and technological progress. . . . The social economy reaches the highest stage of planned organization, and the most effective and rational use is made of the material wealth and labour reserves to meet the growing requirements of the members of society.'

'People's requirements will be satisfied from public sources. Articles of personal use will come into the full ownership of each member of society and will be at his disposal.'

'To each according to his needs'

'In the next decade (1971-1980) the material and technical basis of communism will be created . . . Soviet society will come close to a stage where it can introduce the principle of distribution according to needs.'

'The disparity between high and comparatively low incomes must gradually shrink. Increasingly greater numbers of unskilled personnel will become skilled, and the diminishing difference in proficiency and labour productivity will be accompanied by a steady reduction of disparities in the level of pay. As the living standard of the entire population rises, low income levels will approach the higher, and the disparity between the incomes of peasants and workers, low-paid and high-paid personnel and the populations of different parts of the country, will gradually shrink.'

'At the same time, as the country advances towards communism, personal needs will be increasingly met out of public consumption funds whose rate of growth will exceed the rate of growth of payments for labour. The transition to Communist distribution will be completed after the principle of distribution according to one's work will exhaust itself, that is, when there will be an abundance of material and cultural wealth and labour will become life's prime necessity for all members of society.'

(Note that the New Programme specifies some of the personal needs which will be 'increasingly met out of public consumption funds': education, medical services, housing, transport, holidays, catering, plus the special needs of disabled people, unmarried mothers, students, and the aged.)

Public self-government replaces the state

'Vigorous extension and perfection of Socialist democracy, active participation of all citizens in the administration of the state, in the management of economic and cultural development, improvement of the Government apparatus, and increased control over its activity by the people constitute the main direction in which Socialist statehood develops in the period of the building of communism.'

'As Socialist democracy develops, the organs of state power will gradually be transformed into organs of public self-government. The Leninist principle of *democratic centralism*, which insures the proper combination of centralized leadership with the maximum encouragement of local initiative, the extension of the rights of the union republics and greater creative activity of the masses, will be promoted.'

'Public functions similar to those performed by the state today in the sphere of economic and cultural management will be preserved under communism and will be modified and perfected as society develops. But the character of the functions and the ways in which they are carried out will be different from those under socialism. The bodies in charge of planning, accounting, economic management and cultural advancement, now Government bodies, will lose their political character and will become organs of public self-government. Communist society will be a highly organized community of working men. Universally recognized rules of Communist conduct will be established whose observance will become an organic need and habit with everyone.'

'Historical development is bound to lead to the withering away of the state.'

Willing labour for the good of society

'Thanks to the changed character of labour, its greater mechanization and the high degree of consciousness of all members of society, the latter will work willingly for the public benefit according to their own inclinations.'

'Communist production demands high standards of organization, precision and discipline, which are insured, not by compulsion, but thanks to an understanding of public duty, and are determined by the whole tenor of life in Communist society. Labour and discipline will not be a burden to people, labour will no longer be a mere source of livelihood—it will be a genuinely creative process and a source of happiness.'

The New Programme ends on a note of triumph:

'When the Soviet people will enjoy the blessings of communism, new hundreds of millions of people on earth will say: "We are for communism". It is not through war with other countries,[7] but by the example of a more perfect organization

[7] The Chinese Communist Party differs from the Russian Party concerning war between 'imperialist' and socialist countries. The difference is not (as the Russians claim) that the Chinese regard such war as *inevitable*, but that the Chinese predict a socialist 'victory' if war should come: 'On the debris of a dead imperialism, the victorious people would create very swiftly a civilization thousands of times higher than the capitalist system and a truly beautiful future for themselves' ('Long Live Leninism', in *Essential Works of Marxism*, ed. A. P. Mendel, p. 534).
The Chinese give two reasons for maintaining this:
(i) *Dogma:* 'The possession of nuclear weapons by imperialism has not changed by one iota the nature of imperialism, which is rotten to the core and declining, inwardly weak though outwardly strong; nor has it changed by one iota the basic Marxist-Leninist principle that the masses of the people are the decisive factor in the development of history.' 'All Marxist-Leninists firmly believe that the course of history necessarily leads to the destruction of nuclear weapons by mankind, and will definitely not lead to the destruction of mankind by nuclear weapons' (*The Differences Between Comrade Togliatti and Us,* pp. 21, 14).
(ii) *Tactics:* 'In no circumstances must Communists act as a voluntary propagandist for the U.S. imperialist policy of nuclear blackmail.' 'The more one "shudders" with fear, the more unbridled and the greedier U.S. imperialism becomes, and the more it persists in using threats of nuclear warfare and raising ever greater demands' (*Ibid.,* p. 15).

of society, by rapid progress in developing the productive forces, the creation of all conditions for the happiness and well-being of man, that the ideas of communism win the minds and hearts of the masses.'

'The party solemnly proclaims: the present generation of Soviet people shall live under communism.'

What does the Christian Believe about Property and Economics?

There is no such thing as 'Christian economics'

Before Christian convictions concerning property and economics are set forth, a general comment should be made concerning the outline of Communist convictions.

In any consideration of Communist economics it is important to make a distinction between questions of economic fact and questions of human value. This distinction is alien to Marxists, but it is important for Christians. On the one hand, Communist economics claims to describe the *facts* of economic life; it claims to give a true and accurate account of what has actually occurred or is occurring, and to make thoroughly reliable predictions concerning what is going to occur in the near future. On the other hand, Communist economics is a programme which sets forth what *ought* to be done, and it is an *evaluation* of economic systems in relation to various human values which it assumes.

Facts. Few readers of this study booklet are likely to find the factual claims of Communist economics entirely convincing. Many are likely to protest against what seem to be gross errors or distortions of fact, and in this they have the support of expert non-Communist economists. In this study booklet, however, we shall not attempt to appraise the factual claims of Communist economics. This is a job for the economist, whether he be Christian or non-Christian. One need not be a Christian in order to find Communist economics radically defective as a description and explanation of contemporary economic history. On the other hand, some Christians accept most or even all of the Communist factual claims; if we think that they are mistaken, we must not appeal to their Christian faith but to the detailed evidence which economists consider.

All this means that insofar as economics is a *factual* matter, we cannot compare Communist convictions concerning economics with Christian convictions concerning economics, for there is no distinctively 'Christian' economics to consider. (Similarly there is no distinctively 'Christian' physics or geology or physiology.)

Non-Communist economists, however, would ask questions like these: Is not the economic power of a capitalist *limited* in varying degrees by the power of trade unions or of government regulations? Does capitalism involve extensive exploitation of *female* and *child* labour everywhere today? Does the high standard of living in *all* advanced capitalist countries depend on poverty in underdeveloped countries? Have not the periodic crises of capitalism been brought under *control* by modern monetary policies, deficit government financing, and other devices? Is there a mounting struggle between capital and labour in *all* capitalist countries? Can Communist socialism work efficiently in meeting the needs of *consumers* rather than the earlier needs for industrialization?

These questions will not silence a Communist economist, who will have answers which may seem plausible to some Christians, though not to most. This document, however, is not the place to carry on the debate concerning economic fact.

Values. Although the Christian faith provides no 'Christian economics', it does have distinctive convictions concerning the *attitudes which men ought to have towards property*; also, it provides a basis for setting forth *criteria which an economic system ought to fulfil.* These attitudes and criteria are relevant in *any* society.

We shall first consider Christian attitudes towards property.

Attitudes towards property

'One of the multitude said to him, "Teacher, bid my brother divide the inheritance with me". But he said to him, "Man, who made me a judge or divider over you?" And he said to them, "Take heed, and beware of all covetousness; for a man's life does not consist in the abundance of his possessions"' (Luke 12. 13-15).

The Christian faith is like the reply of Jesus: it does not provide specific solutions to problems of property and economics, but it does promote specific attitudes.

The New Testament teaches Christians to view property as a dangerous source of temptation, a perennial occasion for the sins which destroy right relations with God and with one's fellow men. On the one hand, there are the sins of anxious idolatry and of self-sufficient pride; in each case wealth replaces God as the focus of a man's ultimate concern and the source of his self-esteem. On the other hand, there are the sins of callousness and greed; the pursuit of wealth alienates men from one another, for true fellowship requires mutual concern and commitment. All property should be labelled, 'Handle with Care', for it is dangerous.

Some Christians have tried to avoid the dangerous temptations of property by giving it up. They have discovered, however, that voluntary poverty does not by itself eliminate the temptation to anxiety or greed; and it does not by itself provide a positive solution to the problem. The remedy lies in various biblical attitudes. This 'remedy' is not a cure-all, but it does provide a creative context in which secular scientific knowledge can be applied to specific economic problems. Four biblical attitudes are specially important:

(i) *Detachment*. 'Where your treasure is, there will your heart be also.' If a man values obedience to God and fellowship with him more than any material possessions, he is detached from depending on these possessions for his fundamental happiness. So poverty need not lead to an anxious idolatry of Mammon, and riches need not lead to vain boastings of self-sufficiency. Moreover, whether his material blessings are few or many, he can enjoy them to the full as they come, as gifts from God; his enjoyment need not be spoiled by anxiety or self-assertiveness.

Detachment is a virtue. By itself, however, it might lead to callousness, for a man who can face poverty with equanimity may become indifferent to the poverty of others. M. Richard Shaull has some wise words concerning this: 'If our witness at this point is to be truly Christian, freedom from obsession with material things must be accompanied by the utmost concern for the material well-being of others. The question of bread for me is a material question. The question of bread for my neighbour is a spiritual matter' (M. Richard Shaull, *Encounter with Revolution*, New York, p. 130).

(ii) *Stewardship.* God is the absolute owner of all things. The Christian looks on himself as a steward of whatever social and personal property he 'owns' according to the legal conventions of human society. Property is held in trust from God, and all men are responsible to him. Each property owner is answerable to God for his use of whatever property has been entrusted to him, whether it be producer's goods or consumer's goods. No man or group of men has absolute ownership of property, whether this be land and factory, or home and family car. Moreover, the conventional property rights of owners matter less in the eyes of God than the human rights of the needy. Generosity is justice, for God upholds the right of the needy to the necessities of life.

John Baillie wrote this concerning his Christian childhood: 'I cannot remember a time when I did not already feel, in some dim way, that I was "not my own" to do with as I pleased, but was claimed by a higher power which had authority over me' (*Our Knowledge of God*, Oxford, p. 4). Similarly a Christian will say, 'My property is not my own, to do with as I please', for the property is God's, and God's claim upon it is recognized in the needs of other men.

(iii) *Partiality to the poor.* The prophets revealed God's bias in favour of the poor, his concern for those who lack both personal property and social property. It is true that God loves all men equally, but none the less he is specially concerned for the oppressed and the neglected. In biblical times, the divine partiality was towards widows, orphans, slaves, foreigners, and small farmers endangered by big farmers. In modern times, Christians should be champions of economic under-dogs in every society, whether the society be capitalist or communist.

(iv) *Fellowship-love.* Personal property, when it is shared with other Christians, is a means of expressing Christian fellowship-love. This sharing of consumer's goods has taken various forms, following two New Testament examples: 'consumer communism' (Acts 4. 31-35) and 'mutual aid' (II Cor. 8. 1-5). The source of the impulse to share personal property voluntarily is the Holy Spirit, who binds Christians together not only in a 'spiritual' communion but also in a very 'material' community.

The New Testament examples reveal an attitude of mutual concern and co-operative commitment which ought to be present in Christians; but they do not in themselves warrant *producer* communism (communal ownership of social property, the means of production) or *government-enforced* sharing of consumer's goods. Questions concerning producer communism and concerning the welfare state cannot be settled simply by reference to Acts and 2nd Corinthians. In general, the New Testament itself provides little guidance concerning economic policies for a nation-state, since the writers and readers of the New Testament were not in the position of facing any decisions concerning such matters.

Nor is it helpful to point to later Christian communities which have practised both consumer communism and producer communism. Such groups as the monastic orders in the Catholic tradition and the brotherhood movements in radical Protestantism have been valuable as protests against worldliness and as expressions of Christian fellowship; but their value depended on their being *voluntary* associations *within* the larger society of men. Their rules could not be enforced effectively on society as a whole, and would not rightly be so enforced. Thus although their example is edifying, they do not provide a simple solution to questions of economics in the nation-state.

We have seen that New Testament teaching concerning personal attitudes towards property does not in itself provide a basis for Christian principles in the nation as a whole. This is well illustrated by the principle, 'From each according to his ability, to each according to his need'. The attitudes required of a Christian make this an ideal and a standard of his own personal behaviour. The obligation of stewardship requires, 'From me according to my ability'. The priority of the rights of the needy, God's partiality towards the poor, and the fellowship-love of Christians require, 'to others according to their need'. But does the principle set forth a desirable and attainable goal for a nation-state?

There are other pressing questions which should be faced, as we have seen: Who should own the means of production? Are there any limits on the welfare which the welfare state should provide? And, more fundamentally, what are the *criteria* by which a Christian judges the merits of various economic systems which now exist or which may exist in the future?

No simple appeal to New Testament passages can settle such questions, which go beyond the realm of individual Christian attitudes and economic practices within small Christian fellowships. However, there are Christian convictions concerning the nature and needs of men which have developed during centuries of Christian thought and experience, and these convictions do provide a framework within which Christians can evaluate economic systems.

In setting forth these criteria for appraising economic systems we will not be describing any existing economic system; none of those in the world today fulfil all the criteria. Nor will we be purporting to show *how* these criteria can be fulfilled in practice; that is a matter of practical wisdom in economics, politics and technology. It is easier to state criteria than to bring about their fulfilment in practice. Indeed, the practical problems which are involved in efforts for economic betterment are extremely complex and burdensome. Anyone who is actively wrestling with these problems deserves encouragement rather than the rebuke which may seem to be implied in lofty talk about what would be ideal. Nevertheless it is important that the matter of *goals* in economic life should not be ignored.

We set forth the following criteria for serious consideration.

CRITERIA FOR ECONOMIC SYSTEMS

Efficient production of consumer's goods

(a) *Production of subsistence.* An economic system should enable the existing productive forces of a country to produce enough consumer's goods to meet the minimum material requirements of existence for the population; or it should encourage the rapid development of productive forces which can do so. If a system does not satisfy this criterion, no other special merits can make up for such a radical defect. Man does not live by bread alone, but he must have bread to live.

(b) *Production of affluence.* Beyond meeting the requirements of men for physical existence, an economic system should encourage a gross national product which can provide a 'surplus of goods which alone makes a human civilized life possible' (Emil Brunner). Christians welcome an abundance of consumer's goods, for this makes possible a level of enjoyment and culture for the masses which previously has been the privilege of only a few. Nevertheless the production of affluence is less important than the production of subsistence. Moreover, a system which produces an enormous quantity of goods may have other defects which make a 'human civilized life' virtually impossible—for example, extremes of wealth and poverty, or totalitarian tyranny.

(c) *Production related to genuine needs.* An economic system might produce a great quantity of consumer's goods and yet be inefficient in that it fails to meet many of the real needs and wants of people. There are two main ways in which production may fail to be geared to consumer requirements. On the one hand, socialist central planners may flout consumer requirements by imposing their own ideas of what people need; if the market does not operate so as to reflect consumer preferences, even a well-intentioned bureaucrat may fail to ascertain consumer requirements accurately. On the other hand, capitalist production may aim at 'planned obsolescence' rather than the durable products which consumers want; and capitalist advertising may misrepresent products, create illusory needs and debase public taste.

Just distribution of consumer's goods

Efficient production is not enough. As Pope John XXIII has said, 'The economic prosperity of any people is to be assessed not so much from the sum total of goods and wealth possessed as from the distribution of goods according to norms of justice' (*Mater et Magistra*, # 74).

(a) *Minimum 'floor' for all.* As long as men lack the elementary necessities of life, excessive wealth is unjust, regardless of how it has been acquired. The principle 'to each according to his need' is *prior* to the principle 'from each according to his ability' until the basic needs of the poor are met. This priority is expressed to some extent in the modern states which have a graduated income tax which provides revenue for social welfare.

What constitutes a 'minimum floor' which meets 'basic need'? Obviously this will vary in different countries and it cannot be specified in great detail. However, Pope John XXIII has expressed convictions concerning this matter which deserve serious consideration: 'Every man has the right to life, to bodily integrity, and to the means which are necessary and suitable for the proper development of life; these are primarily food, clothing, shelter, rest, medical care, and finally the necessary social services. Therefore a human being also has the right to security in cases of sickness, inability to work, widowhood, old age, unemployment, or in any other case in which he is deprived of the means of subsistence through no fault of his own' (*Pacem in Terris*, # 11).

What if it *is* a man's own fault, or seems to be? What if a man *will* not work, or cannot hold a job, or is an habitual 'sponger'? It is tempting to quote Paul's injunction, 'If any one will not work, let him not eat'. But although some societies (including Communist 'socialism') vigorously apply this teaching, Christians should not treat it as a rigid economic rule. Paul's statement in its original context was directed to a specific pastoral situation, and it may be a realistic expression of Christian love in relation to some individuals today; but it was not a general pronouncement for society at large. A just society should recognize its responsibility for those who have been emotionally and spiritually crippled as well as for those who suffer from some physical or social handicap.

(b) *Rewards proportionate to community service.* Insofar as basic needs of men are being met, the criterion of 'services rendered' becomes applicable in the distribution of additional consumer's goods. Not only prudence but also *justice* requires that some men should receive more than others for their services to the community. Let us imagine a sinless utopian society where no man would *require* extra material rewards for extra services; surely it would be *just* for this society to try to reward any special contributions to its welfare, even though the reward would probably be graciously declined. Moreover, in all existing societies, a proportionate reward for services rendered is not only just, it is also realistic. Most men *require* such reward as an incentive in their work, though it is not necessarily their only incentive.

The criterion of 'services rendered' must not be misused as an excuse for injustice. It does not warrant such extreme differences of income as exist in most societies today—differences which are out of all proportion to services rendered, and which often have no connection at all with services rendered. Moreover, the criterion means that the minimum floor should *rise* as the national income rises; otherwise extreme differences of income will occur.

(c) *The right to private property.* It is God's purpose that individuals should be able to exercise a right to full possession of some consumer's goods. (We shall consider producer's goods later.) Without this right, a man is not free. As Emil Brunner says, 'The man who has nothing at his disposal cannot act freely. He is dependent on the permission of others for every step he takes, and if they so wish, they can make it impossible for him to carry on any concrete activity. Without property there is no free personal life' (*Justice and the Social Order*, p. 59).

Christians are interested, not in the existence of an abstract right to private property, but in the *exercise* of this right by all men in a society. It is specially important that all men should be able to possess some 'personal belongings' which are almost as intimately related to them as their own limbs.

The right to private property does not rule out the possibility of *voluntary* renunciation of private property by individuals who decide to practise 'consumer communism' in a small community such as a monastic order or a Christian sect. The economic system of the country should give men the *right* to do this if they so choose. On the other hand, an *in*voluntary consumer communism imposed upon men would violate their fundamental rights.

A man's right to own consumer's goods should be distinguished from his right to *use* consumer's goods which are owned by another. In ancient times, a benevolent master might let his slave use his villa. Today, a business corporation or a Communist state may let an individual use its holiday home, saying 'It's yours'. This may be a laudable practice; but it is not a case of private ownership. Everyone should have private possession of *some* things. Nevertheless, not all consumer's goods need be privately owned; indeed, ownership by a group may enable more individuals to enjoy the use of the goods. Whether the group is a co-operative or a corporation, a municipality or a national government, the same question then arises: what democratic powers does the individual have in relation to the group?

This question becomes crucial when we consider group ownership of producer's goods.

Economic democracy and producer's goods

(a) *The basic issue.* Much Christian discussion has been focused on the right to private property. Theologians have disagreed as to whether this is an inalienable right which comes to man from the Creator or a human convention which has necessarily (but regrettably) arisen because of man's fall into sin. This controversy is still important in discussions of private property in *consumer's* goods. (We have come down on the side which maintains a God-given right.) But in relation to *producer's* goods, the primary issue is not ownership but what we shall call 'economic democracy'.

Christian thinkers may picture and applaud a society in which each man owns his own means of production so that the right to private property in producer's goods is fully exercised by everyone. Such a picture, however, is unrealistic in relation to modern industrial forces of production. If capitalism pictures itself in such terms, it is being dishonest, for in practice capitalism does not and *cannot* mean that each and every man owns his own means of production. The typical modern unit of production is not a home-handicraft enterprise or a small family farm but a large factory. In modern industry the private ownership of means of production by one individual precludes private ownership by other individuals. What usually happens is that there is ownership by a *group*—a corporation, a co-operative, or the state. And whether a factory is owned by an individual or a group what matters most is not 'Who holds the legal title to the property?' but 'Who really controls the power-structure in its operations?' Does the individual worker have any power?

Communist replacement of private ownership by public ownership does not automatically give each worker some power within the economic system. Each worker's individual share in the public ownership of producer's goods is tiny; it is comparable to owning one share in General Motors. The crucial question is whether he has democratic rights and opportunities and powers within the decision-making machinery of the economic system.

In some Christian teaching the central economic principle is still 'the right to private property in producer's goods'. Such teaching is misleading. In modern industrial economies only a capitalist minority could actually exercise this right; the majority could not. Although originally the teaching was an attempt to safeguard men against economic tyranny, now it is likely to seem like an attempt to do the opposite. In modern industrial society, Christians who want to be not only faithful to Christian theological convictions but also realistic and relevant should emphasize the need for economic democracy within the economic power-structure of society.

Christian theological convictions concerning the goodness and the sinfulness of man imply the possibility and the necessity of economic democracy. As Reinhold Niebuhr has said in a wider context, 'Man's capacity for justice makes democracy possible; but man's inclination to injustice makes democracy necessary.' The necessity for economic democracy is specially urgent today because the forces of production in modern industrial society tend to bring about dangerous concentrations of economic power. This power is likely to be abused, whether the men who wield it belong to the inter-locking directorates of capitalist big business or to the inner core (the 'aktiv') of the Russian Communist Party.

(b) *The four 'p's' of economic democracy.* Economic democracy depends on what may be called the four 'p's': protection, participation, protest and pluralism.

The individual must have *protection* against arbitrary economic power which can deprive him of his livelihood, regiment his life as if he belonged to an industrial 'army', or otherwise threaten his basic freedom and security. This protection requires an effective legal restraint on economic power.

The individual must be able to *participate* in economic decision-making, especially concerning matters which affect him most immediately, such as conditions of work, wage or salary policies, etc.

It is true that the central administration of a business enterprise or of the national economy cannot be expected to consult every worker concerning every decision. Nevertheless there should be a usable machinery of *protest* whereby individuals and minority groups can bring pressure on the administration to revise general policies. This is analogous to the working of political democracy, which does not presume to settle every matter by a plebiscite, but which has means at its disposal whereby a government can be forced to change general policies and can even be forced to give up its powers.

Pluralism means a diversity of economic power groups within a nation: government, big business, small business, professional associations, trade unions, co-operatives, consumer groups, etc. Although an excessive pluralism may lead to inefficiency in production, an absence of pluralism leads to tyranny. Government ownership of some producer's goods need not lead to tyranny, since the electorate may exert effective political controls on the government. If, however, the government is sole owner of *all* producer's goods in the country, and there are thus no other independent economic groups to check its power, the leaders of government will wield not only economic power but also supreme political power. Those who deny the need for checks on economic power reveal a naïve optimism concerning the idealism of men in positions of unlimited power and concerning the effectiveness of political protest in a non-pluralist economic system. A similar danger of tyranny arises in a capitalist society if monopolies come to dominate its economic life and also (or thereby) gain effective control of the supposedly democratic government.

(c) *Small productive units and co-operatives.* Economic democracy also involves a bias in favour of small productive units and in favour of co-operatives.

Although the productive forces of modern industrial economies do tend to require large units of production for efficient operation, small units should be encouraged wherever they can do as good a job. Small units are beneficial not only in terms of pluralism of power, but also (as we shall see) because of the human values which can more easily be achieved within them.

Producer co-operatives or corporations with profit-sharing and worker-participation programmes should be encouraged, since they are forms of group ownership which deliberately promote economic democracy within an enterprise.

(d) *Economic democracy and economic efficiency.* The democratic benefits of economic pluralism and of other elements in economic democracy must be weighed against the possible productive benefits of highly centralized government control, which may mean effective planning and co-ordination of the national economy. If a country cannot provide even a level of subsistence for its citizens, the need for production under strong government direction may make economic democracy somewhat less important as a criterion. On the other hand, if a country has already achieved a high level of production, it would be tragic for people to sell their birth-right of democratic liberty for an affluent mess of potage.

Two rights: work and education

Traditional Christian teaching has stressed man's *obligation* to work. This teaching is still true and important, but the problem of unemployment in modern capitalist economies has rightly focused attention on man's *right* to work. A society which denies him this right denies him an opportunity to maintain himself and his family by his own labour and an opportunity to contribute to the welfare of society. This can be an affront to human dignity and self-respect which is not satisfactorily remedied by the dole or even by unemployment insurance.

Man has not only the right to work but also the right to education. We agree with Pope John XXIII that man has 'the right to basic education and to technical and professional training in keeping with the stage of educational development in the country to which he belongs. Every effort should be made to ensure that persons be enabled, on the basis of merit, to go on to higher studies, so that, as far as possible, they may occupy posts and take on responsibilities in human society in accordance with their natural gifts and the skills they have acquired' (*Pacem in Terris*, # 13).

Opportunities for work and for education should not depend on race or class. In matters of work or education, any discrimination based on race or class is a violation of human rights.

The right to work and the right to education are specially important in modern industrial society where producer's goods (the means of production) are characteristically owned by groups. The individual must depend on economic democracy within these groups, but he still has his own skill, and this is analogous to private ownership of a producer's good. The right to acquire a skill and to use it gainfully is thus analogous to the traditional right to 'private property in producer's goods'.

In the future, the right to work may become difficult to uphold in economically advanced countries where automation is increasing. There may be few jobs in general, and no jobs at all for some men whose skills are no longer required. If a man cannot *earn* his livelihood, but receives it from the rest of society, must he necessarily lose his human dignity and his sense of worth? *No.* In the past, 'work' has had two elements: earning a living and making a contribution to society. Human dignity and worth can be maintained when only the second element is present. Enforced leisure can be an opportunity rather than a tragedy if men can find unremunerative activity which is nevertheless *creative*: personally meaningful and socially useful. Society should help men to do this, especially by means of adult education which is not necessarily training for *remunerative* activity.

Beneficial side-effects on persons

We have seen that an economic system should satisfy the material and cultural needs of men as consumers and promote their rights as producers. These central purposes of an economic system provide obvious criteria by which it can be appraised. But a system also has side effects which are extremely important. Just as a new drug which cures a disease may have negative side-effects which give it a low overall value, so an economic system may satisfy many of the criteria which we have considered and yet be deplorable because of its side-effects on the moral and spiritual development of men.

Specific economic evils undermine human personality. E. Clinton Gardner gives three examples which John Bennett has noted: 'poor housing conditions, which may have disastrous effects upon family morale and thus adversely affect the emotional health of children in ways that are important for growth in the awareness of God's love; contrasts in a society between extreme wealth and extreme poverty, which may generate bitterness and hostility and constitute a serious barrier to fellowship; unemployment, which creates in the unemployed a sense of not being needed and wanted—a feeling of being rejected by society as well as a feeling of guilt for not being able to provide for one's dependents' (*Biblical Faith and Social Ethics*, p. 284).

Human beings are affected not only by specific economic evils but also by the general structure and atmosphere of an economic system. It is not true that human character is absolutely determined by any economic system. Indeed, some men of spiritual stature transcend their economic environment in remarkable ways. Most men, however, are profoundly influenced by it. Christians should be concerned about five different ways in which this influence is at work:

(a) *Detachment or idolatry*. An economic system influences the attitudes which men have towards property. It is natural and right that men should seek to acquire things and should enjoy using them. But an economic system may stimulate acquisitive greed and pride of possession to an inordinate and idolatrous degree. Instead, it should appeal not only to self-interest but also to altruism, and it should foster more respect for public service than for conspicuous consumption. The practice of Christian detachment is not encouraged in an economic environment which stimulates its opposite.

(b) *Stewardship or irresponsibility*. An economic system may foster irresponsible exploitation of natural resources and irresponsible use of accumulated economic resources. This is not only disastrous for the economic well-being of later generations, it is also destructive in its personal effects on the present generation. People whose motto is 'I'm all right, Jack' lack the mature perspective and social concern which human beings should attain. The practice of Christian stewardship is doubly difficult in an irresponsible society.

(c) *Integrity or Deception*. A man should 'be himself', deceiving neither others nor himself concerning his real convictions and motives. A society in which most human talk and action does not 'ring true' is less than human. Such a society may arise not only because of the wilful hypocrisy of individuals, but also because of the influence of an economic system which requires of men an external and internal conformity to some role or ideology. Capitalist economies require many men who can 'sell' not only goods but also themselves. Communist economies require an ideological uniformity: each and every person must be a keen Marxist-Leninist, regardless of his real convictions and motives.

(d) *Fellowship or impersonality.* Contemporary psychology and Christian theology agree in insisting that mutually responsive human fellowship is essential to the growth of human personality. Such fellowship can be enjoyed in the family or in other small groups, but it should also be fostered in a man's daily work. The economic community in which a man works should, wherever possible, include a group which is small enough for him to know each person in it. This group should be able to co-operate in some decision-making and in mutual concern. Working conditions and methods should be modified whenever possible so as to help people to become more truly human in the give and take of daily encounters. Efficiency of production is very important, but man's need for fellowship should not be completely overridden.

Sometimes an economic system does foster fellowship in these ways, but often it promotes an impersonal and inhuman atmosphere of work. On the one hand, it may encourage men to break up human community by anti-social individualism. On the other hand, it may force men into collective-mass anonymity, each man being merely a cog in the great productive machine.

(Christian concern for fellowship is not sentimentalism. Where there are genuine conflicts of economic interest, the Christian must face the fact and work with others to find a just compromise. Where there is gross injustice, the Christian will seek to reduce bitterness and hatred, but he will work for genuine justice rather than a superficial 'harmony'.)

(e) *Creativity or destruction.* Is a man's work creative in its effect on the man himself? Does he express himself in any way through it? Does he develop himself in any way through it? Has it any meaning for him except as a source of income?

Could it, without false sentimentalism, have any such meaning?

Many jobs in modern industrial society are more destructive than creative; the operations required are monotonous, mechanical and meaningless; the man enslaved to the machine becomes like a machine himself. To some extent this is unavoidable because of modern forces of production. Yet economic systems vary considerably in the extent to which they minimize the destruction of human personality in the work that men must do, and multiply the jobs in which men can find creative self-expression and self-development.

Commentary

This study booklet is not an attempt to give a factual comparison of economic life under Communism (for example in Russia) with economic life in other countries (for example, the USA or India). Such a comparison is important, since it provides the facts on which one can base a realistic appraisal. In this booklet, however, we are interested in the convictions of Christians and Communists; these convictions provide *criteria* for Christian and Communist appraisals of economic systems.

Some Communist convictions should be *rejected* by Christians, some should be *accepted*, and some are *optional* (that is, Christian faith does not imply disagreement or agreement, although Christians may have other reasons for disagreement or agreement).

Disagreements with Communism

(1) Communist convictions involve an *inadequate awareness of the need for economic democracy*. Although Communists are aware of the importance of economic power and the dangers of economic tyranny in capitalistic society, they fail to apply this insight to their own society. The concentration of economic power into the hands of the Communist Party,

with its 'unbounded authority' and claims of infallibility, provides little hope of restraint by the four 'p's' of economic democracy: protection, participation, protest and pluralism. The Party Programme's talk about increased popular control and initiative in the economy indicates a heartening awareness of the problem. But the solution in terms of Lenin's 'democratic centralism' is disheartening, for this principle of 'democracy' within the Communist Party allows only for criticism of *how* policies are carried out; no criticism of the policies themselves is permitted. The Party merely *claims* to represent the will and interests of the proletariat; it does not expose itself to democratic *tests* of this claim.

(2) Communist convictions involve a *black and white dogmatism* which is maintained regardless of different conditions in different countries.

For Christians, 'exploitation' is something which varies in degree, since it has to do with unjust wages and inadequate economic power; in some situations the wages are sufficiently just and the workers' economic power is sufficiently great for there to be nothing to warrant the cry 'exploitation'. Communists, however, proclaim the same 'exploitation' everywhere; and they proclaim the same remedy (public ownership), rejecting all other remedies as irrelevant.

Christians are not committed to any dogma concerning the political structure of all capitalist countries; but Communists insist that a capitalist economy results in a 'dictatorship of the bourgeoisie', regardless of varying developments of proletarian economic, political and legal powers.

Christian convictions do not rule out the possibility that capitalist economies may sometimes be so oppressive that class struggle is legitimate and a just revolution is required; but Communist dogma maintains that this is *always* so.

(3) Communist convictions are *unrealistic concerning human nature*. Communism assumes that its changes in the economic structure of society will bring about radical changes in human personality which can be relied upon in two crucial ways: (i) guaranteeing high-minded benevolence in the Party leaders who apply the dictatorship of the proletariat during socialism,

and (ii) ensuring efficient and vigorous labour during communism, so that neither coercion from a state nor the incentive of proportionate reward will be required. Christians do not believe that human sinfulness can be eliminated or radically reduced by economic changes alone.

(4) Communist theory reveals an *inadequate awareness* of the importance of *personal integrity* and of *human fellowship.* There is much criticism of capitalist 'hypocrisy' and anti-social individualism, but little recognition of the dangers inherent in mass indoctrination and mass collectivism. The economic success of socialism depends on two conditions: universal conformity to the Marxist-Leninist ideology and to the Party line, and a rigorous subordination of families and friendships and fellowships to the impersonal proletarian state. Communist theory recognizes this, but it does not recognize what this may cost in human personality: a nation of slavish conformists whose only inclination is to parrot what the Party says and to do what the Party (Big Brother) commands.

(5) Communist theory *overemphasizes quantity of production* in appraising economic systems. Communists (like many North Americans) tend to think that the productive achievements of an economic system are decisive in demonstrating its superiority.

We have seen that Christians should regard production, especially production of subsistence, as an important criterion. But once the basic material needs of men have been met, other criteria become crucial—for example, the degree of economic democracy. Even a gigantic prison might be efficient in production.

Agreements with Communism

(1) *Just distribution of consumer's goods.* Communist theory envisages a form of socialism in which the distribution of consumer's goods would conform to Christian criteria: a rising minimum floor with a gradual reduction of extreme differences in incomes, but a (subordinate) recognition of the 'services rendered' criterion. This is a just and realistic blend-

ing of 'to each according to his need' and 'to each according to his ability'.

Christians may disagree concerning *whether* such a goal is attainable, and if so, *how* it is attainable (which economic system is most promising). But as an ideal it provides a Christian criterion for appraising existing economic systems.

(2) *Right to work and right to education.* Communist advance under socialism presupposes and ensures a widespread enjoyment of the right to work and the right to education. (Communist success in reducing unemployment and in expanding educational opportunities is so obvious that few would deny it.) On the other hand, Communist theory and practice deliberately deny the rights to 'class enemies', who are granted only the 'right' to the forced-labour camp and its ideological re-education programme. Also, Communist theory and practice require that all education must take place within the rigid framework of Marxism-Leninism: the right to education does not include the right to genuinely free inquiry.

(3) *Partiality to the poor.* In some countries, the Communist Party is one of the few groups which has an active and genuine concern for the plight of the poor. We shall see in Chapter 4 that Christians may sometimes decide not to join forces with the Party even in such situations; Communist theory indicates that Communist policies may be dogmatic rather than realistic and that Communist leaders may be treacherous rather than trustworthy. But a Christian should share in the Communist's attitude of partiality for the poor, which is sometimes more passionate and dedicated than his own—a judgment on his own failure to live up to his faith. On the other hand, in countries where Communists are in power, the Christian may find that his concern for the economic under-dog leads him to defend dispossessed small farmers against Communist bureaucrats.

(4) *Creativity in daily work.* Communist theory postulates a future communistic society in which labour will become a self-expressive and creative activity for all men. Christians may be sceptical as to whether this utopian condition will ever come, but they should agree with the Communist recog-

nition of a basic human need: a man's need to discover and to develop his own creative powers in useful activity. The early Marx stressed this need, and contemporary Communist theory has fortunately not forgotten it.

Christian Options

(1) *Factual claims of Communist economics.* At the beginning of the outline of Christian convictions we noted that the factual claims of Communist economics are not settled by an appeal to Christian faith. In the case of one claim, however, we have seen that Christian convictions are relevant. The long-range Communist prediction concerning a transformation of human nature under Communism depends on a view of human nature which Christians must reject. But all the strictly economic claims deal with matters which call for expertise in economics rather than the wisdom of faith.

It would be misleading to give the impression that the claim of Communist economics to be a science is taken seriously by non-Communist economists. Few would deny that it contains some elements of truth concerning economic processes in the past and the present, and few would deny the moral significance of Communist 'surplus-value' economics as a protest against human inhumanity in capitalism at its worst. But many of the basic Communist dogmas strain the credulity of even a sympathetic reader: increasing misery of the proletariat everywhere, increasing absorption of people into the proletariat everywhere, and increasing inability of capitalism to produce goods. One wonders how many Communists themselves genuinely believe that 'the world capitalist system as a whole is ripe for the social revolution of the proletariat'.[7]

Nevertheless Christians do differ in the degree to which they accept or reject various factual claims of Communist economics. The differences are reasonable, for competent economists also differ, and the economic situation from which Christians speak is different in different countries and different decades.

[7] One difference between Chinese and Russian Communism is that this belief is more alive and operative in the former.

During the American depression of the 1930s Reinhold Niebuhr wrote, 'We are living in a period in which the anarchies of capitalism have reached an insufferable proportion. We cannot go on with the present social organization . . . Fear of disaster ought to drive us towards socialist decision even more than the hope of justice. Capitalism is incompatible with the necessities of a technical civilization' (quoted by C. C. West, *Communism and the Theologians,* p. 126). Such a conviction is not common among Christians in North America today, and Niebuhr himself no longer holds it. It is not uncommon, however, among Christians who live among starving millions in underdeveloped countries and who are impressed by productive successes in Russia and China, perhaps ignoring similar success in Japan.

(2) *Application of Christian criteria.* Christians may agree that all the criteria which we have suggested for appraising economic systems are relevant, and yet disagree with the priorities which we have suggested. Christian economic teaching is not the Gospel, but an attempt to draw implications from the Gospel. It is open to varying interpretations and emphases, and it needs to be constantly revised in relation to changing economic circumstances. Moreover, its application in different countries involves practical judgments in which Christians may disagree even when they agree concerning the basic economic facts of the situation. Hence Christians can and do differ in relation to Communist economic policies.

John Bennett has said, 'There is no Christian economic system. Christianity is older than all existing economic systems. It has no teaching that can be so directly related to the changing conditions of economic life that we can say of any particular economic pattern that it is universally and inevitably Christian. If we were to try to make any system absolute and to give it divine sanction, we would find ourselves in the unfortunate position of all who have tried to freeze history. It is clear that no one of the economic systems that are real alternatives in the world today guarantees all of the values that Christians should seek to conserve' (*Christianity and Communism Today,* London, p. 137).

4

History, Hope and Morality

Communist faith and Christian faith are similar in that each is fundamentally an interpretation of human history on which is based a hope for the future and a morality for the present. But whereas the Communist interprets history in terms of the class struggle, the Christian interprets history in terms of God's action in Jesus Christ.

In Chapter 2 and Chapter 3 we have already indicated various Communist convictions concerning history and the future, since these are central in Communist theory concerning nature, man and God, and concerning economics and property. In this chapter we shall examine these convictions more closely, and the Communist morality which is based on them. Then we shall explore the Christian faith in terms of history, hope and morality. Finally, we shall give a Christian commentary on the Communist view.

What does the Communist Believe about History, the Future and Morality?

HISTORY AND THE FUTURE

(i) *Historical materialism is 'dialectical'*. The historical materialism of Marxism-Leninism sees human history as part of a universal process of cumulative development. Changes in both history and nature are governed by necessary laws which are 'dialectical' in structure.

The word 'dialectic' requires some explanation, since it is a technical term in Communist writing. It comes from the Greek word for 'discussion', and in ancient Greek philosophy it meant a discussion which has three stages: One statement provokes a contradictory statement, and out of the conflict between the two statements there emerges a third statement which reconciles them by drawing forth the partial truths contained in each. In the early nineteenth century, the German philosopher Hegel applied the term 'dialectical' not only to discussion but also to changes in nature and in history. He held that in nature and in history there is a law-observing process whereby one change produces a contradictory change: a 'thesis' produces an 'antithesis' or 'negation'. Then the thesis and antithesis produce a 'synthesis' or 'negation of the negation', which is a further change in nature or history. The threefold pattern is repeated again and again, for each synthesis is itself the thesis for a new antithesis and new synthesis.

Hegel was an idealist, for whom the fundamental reality is mental or spiritual; changes in nature or history—including changes in material reality—arise from a world-Spirit. Marx, however, turned Hegel's dialectic upside-down. He retained the dialectical structure, but he insisted that the fundamental reality is material. For Marx, changes in nature arise from physical causes and changes in history arise from economic factors. Nevertheless, *all* the changes are dialectical in form. 'In Marxist theory the entire development of reality is dialectical, and human history and the laws governing it are only special instances of a universal principle. This gives to the statements of Historical Materialism their note of assurance. Just as the stars and planets have been precipitated from nebular vapour, just as vertebrate animals have developed from unicellular life, so inevitably, will communist society develop out of the contradictions . . . of capitalist society' (J. M. Cameron, *Scrutiny of Marxism,* page 21).

Communists insist that the predictions of Marxism-Leninism do not depend on a mere *assumption* that history always conforms to a dialectical pattern. They claim that Marx discovered immanent and objective laws of historical change, that Marx verified these by reference to the facts of history, and that *thereby* he showed what structure the process has—

a dialectical structure. Critics of Communism reject this claim, but the main point is clear; history is said to be like nature in that it is governed by necessary and objective laws which enable men to make predictions which are not merely probable but *certain.* Thus a Communist does not merely believe or hope that Communism will eventually come; he claims to *know* that it will come. For example, here is a typical quotation from Lenin:

'On the basis of what *data,* then, can the question of the future development of future communism be dealt with?'

'On the basis of the fact that *it has its origin* in capitalism, that it develops historically from capitalism, that it is the result of the action of a social force to which capitalism *gave birth.* There is no trace of an attempt on Marx's part to conjure up a utopia, to make idle guesses about what cannot be known. Marx treats the question of communism in the same way as a naturalist would treat the question of the development, say, of a new biological variety, once he knew that such and such was its origin and such and such the exact direction in which it was changing' (*The State and Revolution,* pp. 144-5).

(ii) *Historical materialism is 'pragmatic'.*[1] Communists insist that theory depends on *practice;* knowledge depends on action and truth is verified by successful achievement.

Marxist-Leninist truth is not discovered merely by passive observation of nature or history; it is discovered by active alteration of nature or history. A man cannot come to know objective laws of nature except by scientific experiment or material production—that is, by changing nature. Similarly, a man cannot come to know objective laws of history except by revolutionary participation in history—that is, by changing society. The test of truth is verification in social practice. We do not prove that *a* causes *b* merely by observing that *a* has always been followed by *b* until now; we need to be able to *bring about b* by producing *a.*

[1] This is not a Communist term and it is associated with the non-Communist philosophy called 'pragmatism'; but it is a useful label for this important element in Marxism-Leninism.

The following quotations from Mao Tse-Tung's famous essay *On Practice* illustrate this fundamental Communist conviction concerning the dependence of knowledge ('cognition') on practice:

'Man's social practice alone is the criterion of truth in his cognition of the external world, for . . . human cognition becomes verified only when it arrives at the results predicted, through the process of social practice, *viz.*, through the processes of material production, of class struggle, and of scientific experiments.'

'Marxist philosophy . . . openly declares itself to be in the service of the proletariat . . . One's theory or cognition is judged to be true or untrue not by how it is subjectively felt to be, but by what objectively the result is in social practice.'

'If one wants to have knowledge one has to participate in the practice of changing existing conditions. If one wants to know the taste of a pear one has to transform the pear by eating it oneself. If one wants to know the composition and properties of atoms one has to perform physical and chemical experiments to change their original state. If one wants to know the theory and method of revolution, one has to participate in revolution.'

'What Marxist philosophy considers most important is not understanding the laws of the external world and thereby explaining it, but actively changing the world by applying the knowledge of objective laws.'
(*On Practice* is in *Essential Works of Marxism,* ed. A. P. Mendel.)

It is important to recognize that Marxism-Leninism is *both* dialectical and pragmatic. On the one hand, the Communist believes that there are objective and necessary laws which govern nature and history. On the other hand, he believes that these laws are discovered and verified by human practice. Thus in relation to the future emergence of communism, the Communist has both a theoretical certainty and a practical commitment; he has both a basis for hope and a basis for action. On the one hand, he is certain that communism will inevitably come, since its emergence from capitalism and socialism is required by the immanent laws of the dialectical historical process. On the other hand, he is committed to participate in this process; he will help to prove that the Marxist-Leninist prediction is true by helping to *make it come true*; his own participation is part of what has been predicted.

Thus a Communist thinks he knows the exact direction in which the historical process is going; this knowledge is derived and tested, not by neutral observation or disinterested reflection, but by participation in the process. Marx summed it up: 'It is not a matter of bringing some utopian system or other into being, but of consciously participating in the historical revolutionary process of society which is taking place before our very eyes' (*Herr Vogt*).

(iii) *History progresses towards freedom.* We have seen that for Communists history is not merely a repetitive or circular process which gets nowhere. The immanent dialectical laws of history show that it has a *direction.* It resembles the actions of a man who is working towards a goal, for it is *progressive.* In the past, this progress has not been deliberately planned by men, but Communists who now participate in history begin to make this progress their own—something which they *will* to bring about. Human history becomes, for the first time, a deliberate production.

Communists measure progress in terms of the growth of human freedom. What do they mean by 'freedom'? Here is Engel's definition:

'Freedom does not consist in the dream of independence of natural laws, but in the knowledge of these laws, and in the possibility this gives of systematically making them work towards definite ends . . . Freedom of the will therefore means nothing but the capacity to make decisions with real knowledge of the subject . . . Freedom therefore consists in the control over ourselves and over external natural necessity; it is therefore necessarily a product of historical development' (*Anti-Duhring*).

When Engels speaks of 'control over ourselves' he is not referring to an individual's self-control, but to the collective control of men over their social, political and economic relations. The economic relationships are, of course, primary. Hence freedom means an increase in the forces of production ('control over external nature'), or an increase in social control over the relations of production ('control over ourselves'). Note that in each case the freedom is *economic* freedom, which for Marxist-Leninists is the precondition of all other freedom, legal, political or personal.

Man first distinguished himself from animals by achieving some degree of mastery over nature. As Engels says, 'The first men who separated themselves from the animal kingdom were in all essentials as unfree as the animals themselves, but each step forward in civilization was a step towards freedom. On the threshold of human history stands the discovery that mechanical motion can be transformed into heat—the production of fire by friction . . . (which) gave man for the first time control over one of the forces of nature, and thereby separated him for ever from the animal kingdom' (*Anti-Duhring*). Similarly, early man discovered how to produce tools, weapons and crops.

The development of such *forces* of production, however, was not an unmixed blessing. It eventually caused a drastic fall in man's control of the *relations* of production. Primitive man had practised communism; that is, the means of production were owned and used communally. Since the technology was primitive, man had little freedom (that is, control) in relation to nature. This made life harsh and difficult, but it also meant that each individual's labour could produce only what was necessary for his own subsistence, and hence there was no possibility of exploitation. Slavery made no sense if a slave could do no more than produce what he himself consumed. When the forces of production increased, however, and surplus value could be produced, the exploitation of one class by another became feasible. The rise of man's freedom over nature brought a fall in man's freedom over himself.

Ever since the fall of man from primitive communism there has been an increase in man's freedom in relation to nature; but man has been in bondage to the relations of production which have developed.

This bondage or lack of freedom has three inter-related elements:

(a) The bondage of the ruled class (slaves or serfs or proletarians) to the ruling class (masters or lords or capitalists).

(b) The periodic bondage of forces of production to outmoded relations of production which lag behind and thwart possible increases in production.

(c) The bondage of society to economic anarchy or planlessness, which means that human history is not a subject of human control.

In previous chapters we examined (a) and (b); but (c) deserves special consideration here. Engels contrasted man's planned activity in relation to nature with his planlessness in relation to society. In relation to nature, man has gradually reduced his subjection to the unintended or unforeseen effects of uncontrolled forces. In relation to society, however, such subjection has increased. 'We find that . . . unforeseen effects predominate, and that the uncontrolled forces are far more powerful than those set into motion according to a plan.' Indeed, 'social production is particularly subject to the interplay of unintended effects of uncontrolled forces and achieves its desired end only by way of exception'. Only conscious organization and planning of social production can 'elevate mankind above the rest of the animal world socially in the same way that production in general has done this for men as a species' (*Introduction to Dialectics of Nature*).

In *Socialism: Utopian and Scientific*, Engels discussed this social or economic bondage more fully, and set forth his remedy:

'With the taking over by society of the productive forces, the social character of the means of production and of the products will be utilized by the producers with a perfect understanding of its nature. . . . Active social forces work exactly like natural forces: blindly, forcibly, destructively, so long as we do not understand and reckon with them. But when once we understand them, when once we grasp their action, their direction, their effects, it depends only upon ourselves to subject them more and more to our own ends. The difference is as that . . . between a conflagration and a fire working in the service of man.'

'With the seizing of the means of production by society . . . man's own social organization, hitherto confronting him as a necessity imposed by nature and history, now becomes the result of his own free action. The extraneous objective forces that have hitherto governed history pass under the control of man himself. Only from that time will man himself, more and more consciously, make his own history . . . It is the ascent of man from the kingdom of necessity to the kingdom of freedom.'

In pre-socialist society, however, 'it is still true that man proposes and God (that is, the extraneous force of the capitalist mode of production) disposes' (*Anti-Duhring*).

Freedom is the power of a *group*. We shall see later that individual freedom is important in the classless society; but in all pre-communist society, freedom belongs either to a class or to society as a whole. As A. L. Morton says, 'A class is free to the extent to which it is able to pursue its proper class interests, and a society is free to the extent to which it is able to understand and control . . . natural forces.'

He goes on: 'For the proletariat after it has seized power, freedom means the freedom to consolidate this power, and to proceed to the further historical stage of the establishment of a classless society. It is free because it is acting in accord with the laws of historical development. But in following its interests as a class the proletariat serves the ends of each individual member of the class.

'In any society divided into classes, freedom for one class inevitably involves the absence of freedom for the classes opposed to it. Under a proletarian dictatorship freedom for the bourgeoisie is just as impossible as is freedom for workers in a bourgeois state. This is a fact which well-meaning people . . . find peculiarly distasteful, and never understand just because they are incapable of perceiving that society is basically composed of classes rather than of individuals. In consequence they fail to grasp the essential dialectic of history, which is the progress towards a classless society through struggle and through the victory of the ultimate exploited class. It is this victory which alone . . . makes possible the emancipation of mankind as a whole, and the possibility of this victory which makes the proletariat the custodian of the future' (*Christianity and the Social Revolution,* pp. 350-53).

Not only does group freedom have priority over individual freedom, *economic* freedom has priority over political and personal freedom. *Only* the achievement of economic freedom (that is, the control of nature and of relations of production) can bring any genuine political and personal freedom. According to Lenin (following Marx), capitalist democracy is a sham. It merely means that 'the oppressed are allowed once every few years to decide which particular representatives of the oppressing class shall represent and repress them in parliament' (*The State and Revolution*). He continues:

'Only in communist society . . . when there are no classes (i.e., when there is no difference between the members of society as regards their relation to the social means of production), *only* then "the state . . . ceases to exist", and it "*becomes possible to speak of freedom*". People will gradually *become accustomed* to observing the elementary rules of social intercourse that have been known for centuries and repeated for thousands of years in all copybook maxims; they will become accustomed to observing them without force, without compulsion, without subordination, *without the special apparatus* for compulsion which is called the state. The expression "the state *withers away*" is very well chosen, for it indicates both the gradual and the spontaneous nature of the process. Only habit can, and undoubtedly will, have such an effect.

'Only communism makes the state absolutely unnecessary, for there is *nobody* to be suppressed—"nobody" in the sense of a *class.* . . . We do not in the least deny the possibility and inevitability of excesses on the part of *individual persons,* or the need to suppress such excesses. But . . . we know that the fundamental social cause of excesses, which consist in the violation of the rules of social intercourse, is the exploitation of the masses, their want and their poverty. With the removal of this chief cause, excesses will inevitably begin to "*wither away*". We do not know how quickly and in what succession, but we know that they will wither away.'

Communists thus claim that freedom over nature (an abundance of consumer's goods) and freedom over history (the abolition of class exploitation) will eventually eliminate both the coercive state and individual 'excess'. That is, it will eventually bring both political freedom and freedom from crime.

Under communism, the collective economic freedoms of men over nature and over history will also enable everyone to achieve a third kind of freedom: *individual* freedom. This has three inter-related elements: freedom in work, freedom in association, freedom from ideology.

(a) *Freedom in work*. Each person will be able to fulfil his various human potentialities in liberating work—work which is not merely a burdensome labour but a creative self-expression, work which is not merely a means of subsistence but an end in itself. Each man as a producer will be creative.

(b) *Freedom in community*. 'Only in community with others has each individual the means of cultivating his gifts in all directions; only in the community, therefore, is personal freedom possible' (*The German Ideology*). In pre-communist societies, the only possible community has been the *class*, which has imposed its own interests upon the individual, so that his mode of life has been moulded by his class membership. Communism, however, is 'an association in which the free development of each is the condition for the free development of all' (*Communist Manifesto*). Genuine individuality is thus possible.

(c) *Freedom from ideology*. In pre-communist societies, ideology and the whole superstructure of social institutions have been the involuntary reflection of class interests as governed by the existing relations of production. Neither human ideas nor human institutions have been genuinely free creations of man. Under communism, however, each man will be freed to view the world realistically and scientifically, and to construct social relations in accordance with his needs and purposes as a man.

In conclusion, we should notice that, according to Communist theory, the progress of history towards freedom has an overall *dialectical* pattern. The 'thesis' was primitive communism, with its meagre forces of production and its necessarily communal relations of production. (These relations were not freely planned; they were virtually instinctive.) The thesis generated an 'antithesis': the era of slavery, feudalism and capitalism, with its expanding forces of production and its necessarily exploitive relations of production. The 'synthesis' will be communism, which deliberately combines the communal relations of production from the 'thesis' and the expanding forces of production from the 'antithesis'. The fall from primitive communism thus eventually makes possible a rise to a higher level of human existence, in which men will achieve freedom over nature and freedom over their own history.

(iv) *Communists participate in the climax of history.* We have seen that for Communists, human history has a beginning, a middle, and an end. The beginning was primitive communism and the end or goal is future communism. The middle is a series of economic systems characterized by class struggles: slavery, feudalism and capitalism. Capitalism is the *last* such system, for its productive forces have given rise to contradictions which make the elimination of classes both possible and necessary. Hence Marx refers to the capitalist epoch as the 'closing chapter of the pre-historic stage of human society'. It is 'pre-historic' in the sense that a genuinely *human* history begins only when men begin to *make* their own history, emerging from the 'kingdom of necessity' into the 'kingdom of freedom'. Their first and fundamental act in moving out of 'pre-history' is to seize the means of production for ownership by society as a whole.

Hence for Communists today, the decisive turning point in history was the Russian Revolution of October 1917, the 'epoch-making turn of mankind from capitalism to socialism' which 'ushered in a new era in the history of mankind, the era of the downfall of capitalism and the establishment of communism' (*1961 Programme of the Communist Party of the Soviet Union*). Nevertheless, capitalism still survives in many countries, and communism has not yet arrived. Hence Communists live in an interim period between the initial victory of communism and its final fulfilment. Communists live during a period when two epochs overlap; the kingdom of necessity persists although the kingdom of freedom has already begun. Communists live during a period in which the final struggle between progressive and reactionary classes is taking place. In previous revolutionary periods, the progressive revolutionary class (for example, the bourgeoisie) was merely a minority. The modern proletarian revolution, however, will bring freedom to the mass of mankind. Victory in this final struggle will mean the end of class struggle and so the end of all war. 'It is we ourselves who with our own hands will put an end to the time of wars in the history of humanity, and the war which we wage is, without any doubt, part of the last war' (Mao Tse-Tung). Indeed, communism means not only the end of war but the end of history as men have so far experienced it and envisaged it. Communism is the goal of this whole historical development, which began with primitive communism.

Nevertheless, communism will not be the temporal end or the ultimate goal of all human history, for it will be the *beginning* of a new age in human progress. Communists do not claim any knowledge concerning subsequent developments during the age of communism. They can only predict that it will begin. Their predictions depend on a knowledge of laws which govern the fall of capitalism and the emergence of socialism with its culmination in communism. Such knowledge provides no basis for predictions concerning changes in communist society, which will have transcended these laws.

During the period of historical climax in which we now live, the proletariat and the Communist Party have a very special role as custodians of the future. This is what Mao Tse-Tung says in *On Practice*:

'At the present stage of the development of society the

responsibility of correctly understanding the world and of changing it has already fallen with the whole weight of history upon the shoulders of the proletariat and its political party. This process of the practice of changing the world on the basis of a scientific knowledge of it has already reached a historic moment both in China and in the whole world, a moment of such importance as the world has never witnessed before. This change is none other than the complete overturn of the world of darkness both in China and elsewhere and the transformation of it into a world of light that never existed before.'

If the proletariat is to fulfil its task of changing the world, it needs to be led by the Communist Party. Lenin insisted that the proletariat needs to be *educated* in Marxism and *organized* for revolution and dictatorship.

Education is required because *spontaneous* proletarian political activity does not promote the true interests of the proletariat. Indeed, 'the spontaneous development of the labour movement leads to its subordination to bourgeois ideology' (Lenin). By itself, the proletariat knows neither its own true interests nor how to further these interests. It is easily deceived by the outward forms of bourgeois democracy or the temporary improvements of bourgeois reformism. It lacks a rational understanding or 'consciousness' of social reality. Members of the Communist Party have a Marxist-Leninist consciousness which must be instilled in the masses of the proletariat. The spontaneous and unreflective feelings and actions of the masses will not by themselves produce either successful revolution or successful socialism. The party must propagate its 'scientific knowledge' of nature and society, for only such Marxist-Leninist knowledge will enable the proletariat to achieve collective freedom (that is, control) over nature and society. The proletariat can only be the 'custodian of the future' if the Party is the faithful custodian and teacher of Marxism-Leninism.

Organization is required because successful proletarian revolution and proletarian dictatorship depends on *power*, and power depends on *unity* of action. The Party organizes the millions of workers into an 'army' of which it is the 'vanguard' (leading division) and the 'general staff'. Class war cannot be waged effectively by a rabble. In capitalist countries, the only weapon of the proletariat against police repression is organization by the Party. Similar organization is still needed in socialist countries, for the continuous struggle against internal and external class enemies. Moreover, organization is required under socialism if there is to be a unified collective control (that is, freedom) whereby the proletariat can effectively impose its own plans on nature and on society.

The internal organization of the Party and the Party's organization of the proletariat are governed by two principles, 'democratic centralism' and 'partisanship'.

According to Lenin, the principle of democratic centralism means 'freedom of criticism . . . as long as this does not disrupt the unity of action already decided upon' and 'the intolerability of any criticism undermining or obstructing the unity of action decided on by the party'. No 'factionalism' is allowed. That is, only individuals have this freedom of criticism; the formation of dissenting groups is prohibited.

The principle of partisanship means that all activities of individuals must be subordinated to the discipline of the Party and the interests of the class struggle. This applies not merely to political activity in the usual sense of the word 'political'. It applies to the whole of life: academic research and family life, art and work, education and sport. Under socialism, Party organization permeates all the organized life of society.

MORALITY

(i) *The essentials of Communist morality.* Communist morality is an inseparable part of the Communist view of history. We have seen that this is not a matter of neutral observation or disinterested reflection, but of 'consciously participating in the revolutionary process of society which is taking place before our very eyes'.

Hence Communist morality has one simple criterion. As

Lenin said, 'Our morality is entirely subordinated to the interests of the class-struggle of the proletariat'. Our morality is derived from the interests of the class-struggle of the proletariat' (*Address to the Russian Youth Communist League, 1920*).

No other criterion is relevant, because a *human* morality as distinct from a *class* morality is impossible until communism has been achieved. As Engels said, 'A really human morality which transcends class antagonisms and their legacies in thought becomes possible only at a stage of society which has not only overcome class contradictions but has even forgotten them in practical life' (*Anti-Duhring*).

The immediate and essential goal in the class-struggle is social ownership of the means of production under the leadership of the Party. Since this eliminates the decisive cause of moral evil in society, its achievement and preservation by proletarian revolution and dictatorship is an end which justifies any means which genuinely promote it. The only limits on such means as violence, treachery, or injustice to individuals, are limits of practical expediency. These limits are important, however, for excess or ineptitude may harm rather than help the proletariat in its class-struggle.

Morality is a part of the super-structure of society. It is a human creation which reflects class interests. Engels says, 'We therefore reject every attempt to impose on us any moral dogma whatsoever as an eternal, ultimate, and forever immutable moral law on the pretext that the moral world too has its permanent principles which transcend history and the differences between nations. We maintain on the contrary that all former moral theories are the product, in the last analysis, of the economic stage which society had reached at that particular epoch. And as society has hitherto moved in class antagonisms, morality was always a class morality; it has either justified the domination and the interests of the ruling class, or, as soon as the oppressed class has become powerful enough, it has represented the revolt against this domination and the future interests of the oppressed. That in this process there has on the whole been progress in morality, as in other branches of human knowledge, cannot be doubted. But we have not yet passed beyond class morality' (*Anti-Duhring*).

Communists insist that their own morality is neither hypocritical nor ineffective nor eternal.

Communist morality is not hypocritical. It does not pretend to be derived from some source outside of human society—from God or from an eternal moral law. Communists openly derive it from the interests of the proletariat.

Communist morality is effective, unlike moralities which appeal to God. Lenin said that God could not create the organization and unity which was required for the overthrow of the unjust social order in Russia. What God could not do, the trained proletariat did.

Communist morality is not eternal. It is the morality of men who live during this present climax in human history. 'That morality which contains the maximum of durable elements is the one which, in the present, represents the overflow of the present (and so) represents the future' (Engels in *Anti-Duhring*). The interests of the proletariat are the interests of mankind, for it is the class which will end all classes.

Communist morality changes during the period of transition from socialism to communism. 'The sphere of action of the moral factor expands and the importance of the administrative control of human relations diminishes accordingly . . . Communism makes the elementary standards of morality and justice, which were distorted or shamelessly flouted under the power of the exploiters, into inviolable rules for relations both between individuals and between peoples. Communist morality encompasses the fundamental norms of human morality which the masses of the people evolved in the course of millenniums as they fought against vice and social oppression' (*1961 Programme of the Communist Party of the Soviet Union*). The *Programme* set forth the following moral code for the 'builder of communism':

'Devotion to the Communist cause, love of the Socialist motherland and of the other Socialist countries;

Conscientious labour for the good of society—he who does not work, neither shall he eat;

Concern on the part of everyone for the preservation and growth of public wealth;

A high sense of public duty, intolerance of actions harmful to the public interest;

Collectivism and comradely mutual assistance: one for all and all for one;

Humane relations and mutual respect between individuals —man is to man a friend, comrade and brother;

Honesty and truthfulness, moral purity, modesty and guilelessness in social and private life;

Mutual respect in the family, and concern for the upbringing of children;

An uncompromising attitude to injustice, parasitism, dishonesty and careerism;

Friendship and brotherhood among all peoples of the USSR, intolerance of national and racial hatred;

An uncompromising attitude to the enemies of communism, peace and the freedom of nations;

Fraternal solidarity with the working people of all countries, and with all peoples.'

All these principles are subordinate to the first: 'devotion to the Communist cause.' The following is Mao Tse-Tung's picture of the dedicated Communist:

'A Communist should be frank, faithful and active, looking upon the interests of the revolution as his very life and subordinating his personal interests to those of the revolution; he should, always and everywhere, adhere to correct principles and wage a tireless struggle against all incorrect ideas and actions, so as to consolidate the collective life of the Party and strengthen the ties between the Party and the masses; and he should be more concerned about the Party and the masses than about the individual and more concerned about others than about himself. Only thus can he be considered a communist' (*Combat Liberalism,* which is in *Essential Works of Marxism,* ed. A. P. Mendel).

(ii) *The ideological enemies of Communist morality.* Communists are committed to an active ideological struggle against various moral views which may seem to be compatible with Marxism-Leninism but which actually support the interests of the capitalists in the class struggle.

(a) *'Liberalism'* is an individualistic claim to a private freedom which is independent of its effects on the Communist cause. Mao Tse-Tung denounces eleven kinds of liberalism. Here are the first and sixth:

'Although the person concerned is clearly known to be in the wrong, yet because he is an old acquaintance, a fellow townsman, a schoolmate, a bosom friend, a beloved one, an old colleague or a former subordinate, one does not argue with him on the basis of principles but lets things slide in order to maintain peace and friendship.'

'Not to dispute incorrect opinions on hearing them, and even not to report counterrevolutionary opinions on hearing them, but to bear with them calmly as if nothing had happened' (*Combat Liberalism*).

(b) *'Objectivism'* is an individualistic rejection of Communist partisanship as it applies to truth. A man claims to know an objective truth which is independent of his class interest and ideological viewpoint and he asserts this alleged truth regardless of its effects on the Communist cause. Marxism-Leninism insists that only Communist practice ensures genuine objectivity. There is no neutral position from which genuinely objective judgments can be made. All non-Communist claims to truth are corrupted to a greater or lesser extent by bourgeois ideology. 'Objectivism' is impossible even in natural science; it is a specially dangerous illusion in morals and politics. Moreover, the truth of a moral judgment or of a political observation is not separable from the effect of *making* the judgment (that is, its effect on the Communist cause). 'The revolutionary practice of millions of people is the only standard for measuring truth' (Mao Tse-Tung).

(c) *'Idealism'* as a moral viewpoint has many versions, but in all of them an action is not judged according to its practical results but according to some other criterion. Some idealists stress motives: love rather than hate, duty rather than self-interest. What really matters, however, is the results of the action in relation to the Communist cause. Some idealists judge actions in relation to abstract and remote *ideals* or *laws*. This leads them to condemn Communist practice on the ground that although the ends are good, the means cannot be condoned. But Marxist-Leninists 'refuse to accept any ethical system that places general principles such as "Thou shalt not steal", "Thou shalt not kill", above the welfare of human beings living in society. The Soviets, for example, in collectivizing agriculture, had to sacrifice a good deal, and many people suffered great privations as a result of the tremendous movement for collectivization. This was sad and tragic, but it is little to pay for the prize of no more famines, no more hunger for nearly two hundred millions of people' (H. Selsam, *Socialism and Ethics*, p. 211).

Idealists do not realize that moral ideals and laws are human products which should be *used* purposefully by men:

' "The sacredness of personality", "the higher things of life", "individual freedom", "inviolability of contracts", "discipline and hardness of character", "sanctity of the home"—these are a few of the idealistic slogans invoked whenever it becomes necessary to protect vested interests against radical change. Each one of these phrases expresses something which is or has been a positive good under definite conditions . . . Their strength and their weakness consist in this: They may serve a progressive function one moment, a reactionary purpose the next—they do not provide, in their idealistic context, any concrete criterion by which their service to men under given conditions may be evaluated' (*Socialism and Ethics*, p. 79).

Pacifism is a form of idealism which must be opposed by Marxism-Leninism. Engels and Lenin pointed out that force has been the 'mid-wife' and the surgical instrument whereby each economic system has given birth to a new and better one. But Communists do not glorify force or idolize it, as Fascists do. No more force is to be used than is strictly necessary for the furtherance of proletarian interest in the class struggle. Indeed, the responsibility for Communist violence lies with the capitalist reactionaries who will not yield their obsolete power peacefully. Communists must not succumb to pacifist idealism, which merely serves the capitalist cause. The goal of universal peace in the future cannot be achieved unless the proletariat is willing to fight for it now. The goal must not become a reactionary ideal which impedes this fight.[2]

(iii) *What Communist morality is not*. Critics of Communism often miss their target because they are attacking something other than the theory of morality which Communists avow. Marx and Engels explicitly repudiate the following views:

(a) *Hedonism* has for its sole goal the enjoyment of physical and sensual pleasures. Marx expressed profound contempt for this individualist obsession with pleasure. Communism looks forward to material abundance for the masses, but not as a primary goal; it is a precondition of human freedom and creativity. Communist sexual morality involves a disciplined subordination to the Communist cause. (To many Western observers, Communist practice even seems puritanical.)

(b) *Utilitarianism* sets forth one criterion for morality: the greatest good of the greatest number. Marxism-Leninism approves its emphasis on results and sometimes seems to argue in the same way, for the proletariat does form the 'greatest

[2] In China under Mao, unqualified opposition to liberalism, objectivism and idealism is required, as it was in Russia under Stalin. Elsewhere, however, contemporary Communist theory is becoming slightly less rigid in these matters. This new trend towards flexibility is evident in *A Philosophy of Man* by Adam Schaff (London, 1963). Schaff, a Polish Communist, still regards *liberalism* as an ideological enemy, but he insists that individual freedom should not be restricted beyond what is genuinely necessary for the development from socialism to communism. He is still opposed to *objectivism* concerning matters which have an ideological content, but he claims that some matters have no such content, for example, mathematics and physics; questions in these areas should be resolved by specialists, not by Party theoreticians. He is still opposed to *idealism*, but he maintains that idealism is right in so far as it holds that there are human needs—and hence human values—which are common to *all* forms of social life. In general, he stresses the need to judge Communist means in relation to 'humanistic' Communist goals. (D. E.)

number'. But utilitarianism has no satisfactory answer to the question, 'What is the "greatest good"? Marxism-Leninism answers this question by reference to the progressive processes of *history*.

(c) *Egalitarianism* sets forth human equality as the fundamental principle of morality, and insists on equal shares for all men in the fruits of production. Marxism-Leninism, however, sets forth proletarian class-interest as the fundamental principle, and is more interested in bigger 'fruits' than in equal slices. Egalitarianism is an individualistic bourgeois ideal. If proletarians try to achieve equal shares for all men under a capitalist system, they merely slow down the class struggle and help the capitalists. The only important equality is equality of status in relation to the means of production and equality of freedom in the classless society.

(d) *Relativism* is the view that all behaviour and belief is relative to the culture in which men live, so that there is no basis for judging that one moral code is better than another. Marxism-Leninism, however, insists that there has been progress in morality, just as there has been progress in science. In both cases, the progress is towards greater and greater freedom. Communists insist that this progress and its criterion are discerned in a scientific study of historical processes.

(e) *Determinism* is the conviction that all human beliefs and actions are determined by inexorable necessary causes, so that freedom is illusory and morality is meaningless. Marxism-Leninism, however, maintains that men can transcend this causal system while nevertheless remaining part of it. Men can *master* both nature and history by coming to know their laws and making them work towards human ends. Both freedom and morality are a conscious participation in history.

Epilogue

What society comes after communism? Communists do not claim to know. Engels, however, ventured a prediction beyond that society. One day there will be no human society at all, for the earth will have become uninhabitable.

Can hope extend beyond the time when mankind is dead?

Yes. Engels found a basis for hope in the eternity and creativity of *matter*: 'We have the certainty that matter remains eternally the same in all its transformations, that none of its attributes can ever be lost, and therefore, also, that with the same iron necessity with which it will again exterminate on the earth its higher creation, the thinking mind, it must somewhere else and at another time engender it' (*Introduction to the Dialectics of Nature*).

What does the Christian Believe about History, the Future and Morality?

We have seen that the basic Communist conviction concerning history and morality is expressed in these words:
'It is not a matter of bringing some utopian system or other into being but of consciously participating in the historical revolutionary process of society which is taking place before our very eyes.'

We shall see that the basic Christian conviction concerning history and morality might well be expressed in these words:
'It is not a matter of bringing some utopian system or other into being but of consciously participating in God's historical activity in Jesus Christ which is evident to the eyes of faith.'

HISTORY AND THE FUTURE

(i) *God's activity in Jesus Christ*. Christians believe that God was at work in the historical man Jesus of Nazareth and that he has continued to work through the risen Jesus in human history until today. This activity of God is only evident to those who have the eyes of faith: that is, those who have been inspired by the Holy Spirit to see it and to participate in it.

Christians believe that Jesus was and is both human and divine. This conviction arose in response to the earthly life of Jesus and then to his risen life within the Christian Church. Jesus of Nazareth was fully human. He shared all the limita-

37392

tions of humanity, yet he was without sin. This meant, positively, that as a man he was unique in three respects. First, his own actions, while remaining fully his own, were also fully God's actions. His obedience was perfect. His words and deeds were divine. Second, his humanity was the perfect expression of God's divinity: that is, his life was the perfect expression or revelation of the love and glory and holiness of God. Third, he rightly claimed divine authority over men, even the authority to forgive sins done to others.

After Jesus was raised from the dead, and made himself known to his followers in various ways, they began to think of him not only as the perfect medium of God's personal action, self-expression and moral sovereignty, but as the presence of God himself. They believed that the risen Jesus was still human, although with a spiritual body, but they acknowledged him as Lord. If the early Christians asked themselves, 'Who is the divine power at work within me, so that my words and deeds are not only mine but also his?', they answered, 'the risen Jesus'. If they asked themselves, 'To whom is glory rightly ascribed in worship?' they answered, 'the risen Jesus'. If they asked themselves, 'Who claims me as his own, directing and ruling my life?', they answered, 'the risen Jesus'.

Christians believe that God was supremely at work in the life and death and resurrection of Jesus. In these historical events, the decisive victory over guilt and sin and death has been won by Jesus. The rest of mankind can participate in this victory for themselves by self-identification with the risen Jesus. The Christian life is a life 'in' Jesus Christ, a participation in what Christ has done and is doing among men. A man who is 'in Christ' can respond to God's forgiveness, God's love and God's resurrection-power, for these are already secretly at work within him. He is called to 'become what he is', to become what God has already done for him and in him. 'As ye have therefore received Christ Jesus the Lord, so walk ye in him' (Col. 2. 6).

A man receives the Lord Jesus Christ, not as an isolated individual, but as a member of Christ's body, the Church. Christ comes to him in the preaching of the Gospel, in the

Lincoln Christian College

sacraments of Holy Baptism and Holy Communion, and in the lives of his fellow Christians. Moreover, he not only receives Christ *through* the Church, he 'walks' in Christ *within* the Church, for he is called to share in the work of the Church. This work is to proclaim and to continue what God began in Jesus Christ.

Nevertheless, Christ is not confined to the Church. Christ comes to the Christian in the needy man whom he helps and in the man who helps him. Also, Christ is Lord and Saviour of all men, not merely of those who are conscious of him. Moreover, the Church is not itself Christ; although it is the body of Christ, it is a fellowship of forgiven *sinners*. Divine judgment begins at the house of God.

Participation in God's activity in Christ is a response to his forgiveness, his love, and his power over death. What is this response?

Christians respond to God's forgiveness by having faith in it and by realizing their constant need of it. This response is vividly expressed by an East German pastor, Johannes Hamel in a lecture to East German students:

'Who are we in comparison with others who do not know God's truth or who even mock and ridicule it? We are people who live on the truth that God in an incomprehensible way has loved us, although we have really earned the opposite. We have enough to do asking God to forgive our own sins. What right have we to look down on those who, in the blindness of their godless hearts, regard God as nothing? . . . Do we Christians in East Germany not involve ourselves in continuing guilt when we criticize with merciless sharpness the evil around us (usually in secret since we are afraid to do it openly), and thereby dismiss those "others" who are guilty of it? In comparison we believe ourselves to be better than those who oppress us. But will God ask us about the evil deeds of others in the Last Judgment, or will he ask us what we have done and what we deserve? We cannot wash ourselves clean with the evil of others' (*A Christian in East Germany*, pp. 94-5).

Christians respond to God's love by trying to share in its expression to other men. This is what Christ empowers the Church to do in the world. We quote again from Hamel:

'Are not those others before whom we are afraid also our neighbours? Don't we live together with them even when we are fighting for our very existence against them? Do we love them with the love of Jesus? . . . The people about us are not given to us so that we may hate them and battle with them. We should neither be indifferent to them nor be afraid of them . . . That a man loves means that he is no more turned in on himself, that he no longer struggles for an idea, a doctrine or a world view, thereby forgetting his fellow-man. To love means that we look at and honour our actual neighbour as the man who carries God's image; that we accept and receive him as one for whom Jesus Christ gave up his life. This is the man for whom it is right to hope that the Holy Spirit will bring him to praise, confession, witness and finally to love . . . Jesus loved these godless enemies of God. Should not we love them?' (pp. 96-7).

Christians respond to God's power over death by facing the finality of death with a hope based entirely on him. Helmut Gollwitzer says this concerning the Crucifixion and Resurrection of Jesus Christ:

'Henceforth from this One who was buried there falls upon our own death a great shadow and a radiant light. A *shadow*—for this we learn in the death of Jesus Christ: he who is dead is really, irrevocably, *dead*. Death in itself is not, as our poets would like to think, a fulfilment. It is a tearing away, a breakdown, a condemnation, which makes all life lose its meaning. It is "the wages of sin". *A bright light*—for here we learn for our own death, from the death of Jesus, the song, of praise: "I shall not die but live". When we go into the grave with him, with Christ himself, we are not alone—there, where man is so utterly alone and so lonely . . . So our hopelessness becomes a preparation for a hope, our grave a sign of life—because even in the grave we have communion with Jesus Christ' (*The Dying and Living Lord,* London, 1960, pp. 90-91).

The Christian hope, however, is not focused primarily on the survival of the *individual* after death. It is true that, after death, the individual Christian will be with Christ; but his 'spiritual body' or personal mode of existence will be incomplete. In biblical thought, the *body* represents, not individual isolation, but solidarity with mankind and with nature. No one can be fully grown in Christ apart from other Christians, or indeed apart from mankind and the whole of creation. The Christian hope for the resurrection of the body is a corporate and cosmic hope. It is focused on the End of history, on the final resurrection. This will involve a transformation of humanity and of nature, a 'resurrection of the whole body and texture of history, a justification of the whole work of God' (J. A. T. Robinson).

Indeed, all that we have said about participation in God's work in Christ must be understood in the context of the biblical view of human history and its conception of the End.

(ii) *The biblical view of human history.* The fundamental biblical conviction concerning God is that he is a personal being who reveals himself through what he *does*, through his mighty acts in *history*. This conviction means that the essential nature of God will be fully revealed in the culmination of history. We quote from J. A. T. Robinson's *In the End, God*:

'Whereas to the Greek the essential was what is true *timelessly*, to the Hebrew it was what still holds true *at the end of time*. For the Bible, the eternal is that which abides, which outstays everything else . . . The end, rather than the non-historical, is what expresses the complete and perfect will of God. Consequently, to see in history the hand of the eternal is to see in history the mark of the *eschaton* (that is, the Last day or the End).

'Just as every historical event which embodies the eternal must in a measure be eschatological, so conversely, the last Divine event, the *eschaton*, must in some sense be historical. This, again, was a necessary conclusion from belief in a God who was a God of history. To the Hebrew mind, the expression of the most real was not timeless essence, but historical event . . . What God is, is what in history he asserts himself to be. Consequently, the ultimate truth about God is necessarily the final event in history' (pp. 36-7).

The conviction that God reveals himself in history was basic in the faith of Israel, for this faith arose in response to an historical event: God's creation of Israel as a people. God had miraculously rescued the Israelites from slavery in Egypt, bringing them safely to the promised land of Canaan; and he had initiated a covenant with them, by which their institutions as a nation were established. In these historical deeds of Exodus and Covenant he had revealed his righteousness and his steadfast covenant-love, and he had chosen Israel to be his obedient servant, the conscious instrument of his purposes for all mankind. Then, when Israel turned away from God, breaking his covenant by committing idolatry and injustice, God revealed his righteousness in judgment rather than salvation. He had chosen Israel for responsibility, not for special privilege; so his judgment was revealed in various catastrophes and supremely in the Exile of Israel to Babylon. However, his salvation was also soon revealed in various recoveries, and supremely in the Return from Exile, which was a sort of Second Exodus.

God's action in history was not confined to Israel. He acted through Nebuchadnezzar of Babylon to bring judgment (Exile) upon Israel, and through Cyrus of Persia to bring salvation (Return). Neither agent acknowledged God, but both were used by him as unwilling and unwitting instruments of his purpose. Neither agent was superior to Israel in righteousness, but God integrated the actions of sinful men into his own purpose. Nor was Israel alone in receiving divine judgment; other nations were also punished for their sins.

The main focus of revelation, however, was the sacred history of Israel. This had a two-fold pattern. On the one hand, there was a repetitive see-saw pattern of salvation and judgment. On the other hand there was a progressive movement in understanding of the End, in which God's purposes would be accomplished and his nature fully revealed.

The see-saw pattern begins with a divine act of salvation,

when Israel is humble, penitent and merciful: receptive to the covenant-mercy of God. Then, however, the success or worldly glory of Israel leads her to be proud, brazen and righteous: rebellious against the covenant-law of God. So judgment comes: Israel is punished for her sins. The punishment is not merely retributive; it is a reformative discipline. Israel learns humility and mercy, and God's salvation comes to her again.

The progressive pattern did not consist of a steadily improving accomplishment of the divine purpose in Israel's actual mode of life. Though there was progress in this, there was also regress—the see-saw pattern of salvation and judgment. Rather, the progressive pattern was in the prophetic vision of what the ultimate accomplishment of the divine purpose would be, in the End. As successive prophets interpreted the Exodus and the subsequent events in Israel's history, there was a progressive heightening in their understanding of the End towards which God had been working and was still working. By the time of the Exile the prophetic vision of the End was very different from the popular idea which Amos had denounced, the idea that God was automatically on Israel's side, and that his purpose was merely to give her victories over political enemies. In Second Isaiah's vision, God's purpose is that *all* men should acknowledge him as King, not only in their worship but in their mode of life, which should express his righteousness. And Israel would become the medium of God's salvation and revelation, not by military victories and worldly glories, but by vicarious suffering on behalf of all mankind.

By the time of Jesus, the contrast between existing historical realities and God's final purposes had become so extreme that many Israelites lost hope for this world—that is, for this Age, which seemed to be a kingdom of evil. Apocalyptic writers had visions of a New Age which would be brought in, not by God at work *through* men, but by God's action alone. The Kingdom of God would replace the kingdoms of this world. This present Age would be replaced by the Age to Come.

'The *New Testament* message is that Jesus is the final revelation of the Divine nature, the last word of God and about God. This means that he is also . . . the last word about history; in him "the time is fulfilled" (Mark 1. 15) . . . The *eschaton* has arrived. The last times have begun, the powers of the age to come have broken in upon the present order. In the person and work of Christ the kingly Rule of God is already a present reality: "If I by the finger of God cast out devils, then is the Kingdom of God come upon you" (Luke 11. 20)' (*In the End, God,* p. 56).

'The function of the imagery of the "last day" is to indicate in unmistakable idiom the *finality* of the processes of life and death, salvation and judgment, already set in motion by the events of the Incarnation . . . But, again, though this finality is stressed in various ways and in various degrees by the whole witness of the New Testament, it is also never forgotten that the present situation is one in which the Rule of God has not yet completely superseded the powers which control this age . . . Christians, as those who belong to the new and yet who still inhabit the old . . . are those upon whom the "ends of the ages" have overlapped' (pp. 59-61).

Hence Christians hold that the New Age is, in all its aspects, both a present reality and a future hope. The End has come, yet it has not come.

The End has come. 'The Second Coming has happened in the return of Christ in the Spirit; the Resurrection of the Body has occurred in the putting on of the new man in the Body of Christ; the Millennium has been inaugurated in the reign of Christ in his Church on earth . . . the Messianic Banquet is celebrated whenever the wine is drunk new in the Kingdom of God; Satan falls from heaven as each man decides for the Gospel, and in the finished work of Christ the prince of this world has been judged; the Last Assize is being accomplished in every moment of choice and decision; Christ is all in all, since all things *have been* reconciled in him' (pp. 66).

The End has not come. 'The New Man from heaven is still "He that shall come"; the Resurrection of the Body will not occur till the final day; for the reign of Christ on his earth men must continue to watch and pray; . . . the Messianic Banquet awaits the Consummation of the Kingdom, and for Satan's overthrow the cry still goes up "How Long?"; the Last Judgment cannot be declared till all consequences are known, and we see not yet all things subjected to Christ' (pp. 66-7).

The Christian hope is that the New Kingdom of Christ will triumph over the kingdoms of this Age. The Christian hope is that what God did in Jesus Christ and what God is doing in Christians will be fulfilled in the End. The basis of this hope is a hidden mystery: 'Christ in you, the hope of glory' (Col. 1. 27).

But how is this hope related to the processes of history as these can be observed by all men? Christians believe that they live in the period of overlap between the Old Age and the New. But has there been any *progress* during this period? Will there be any progress in the future?

We have seen that the Christian hope is a hope *in Christ* concerning life after death and, even more, concerning the End of history. But is it also a hope for progress *along* history? Will the present Age gradually be overcome and displaced by the Age to Come?

(iii) *Christians and progress in history.* If we are to answer these questions, we must first consider what Christians believe concerning the End. Three basic New Testament convictions are involved:

(a) *Death will be abolished.* In the End, death will not merely be overcome, as it was when the dead Jesus was raised by God to new life; it will be abolished. There will be no more death to overcome. Similarly there will be no more suffering or sorrow.

(b) *All history will be fulfilled.* In the End, not only the last existing generation of men but *all* generations will somehow be gathered together. All that has been of genuine value in all human lives will have been preserved by God, even when it had been lost by men in the ongoing processes of history.

(c) *Humanity and nature will be transformed.* In the End,

all evil in humanity and in nature will be either reconciled (and thereby transformed into good) or destroyed. All men will either be transformed into the likeness of Christ or they will be lost. (Universal salvation is a Christian hope, but not a Christian certainty.) Nature will be released from its bondage to futility and decay and will share in 'the glorious liberty of the children of God' (Rom. 8. 21). The whole creation will be united in Christ.

Can there be progress towards the End? Obviously not, in relation to (a) and (b). There are two reasons for this. First, progress is a matter of degree, of closer and closer approximation to some goal; but *either death is abolished or it is not,* and *either all history is fulfilled and stopped or it is not.* Second, *God alone* can abolish death and fulfil history; it is not a matter of God working *through men* to achieve this.

Can there be progress towards the End in relation to (c), the transformation of humanity and nature? Such progress is not *obviously* impossible. Gradual progress towards this end is not an impossible notion, and such progress could conceivably come as God works through men.

It is important, however, to distinguish between hope for the transformation of humanity and nature as part of the *End*, and hope for *progress* towards this transformation. Hope concerning the End (or any element in the End) neither implies a hope of progress nor contradicts it. Two different kinds of hope are at stake here: a 'certainty-hope' concerning the End. and a 'probability-hope' concerning progress.

The distinction between certainty-hope and probability-hope is difficult but crucial. Hope is always an attitude towards something in the future, but there is a difference here not merely in *degree* of hope, but in *kind* of hope. A certainty-hope is a conviction that something cannot fail to happen. A probability-hope is an assurance that something will probably happen.

A Christian certainty-hope depends entirely on faith in God, and it is focused on an End which God alone will bring about. It cannot be falsified or undermined by future events in history; it cannot be made more or less probable by the course of events.

A Christian probability-hope depends not only on faith in God and in God's future actions during the course of history, but also on a consideration of other factors or evidence. For example, to what extent will men respond to God's actions? Or, how likely is it that modern science will bring overall improvement rather than disaster to mankind? Or, has there been progress in the past which provides inductive evidence for predicting probable progress in the future?

A Christian certainty-hope concerning the End is not open to revision in the light of such considerations or because of unexpected historical developments. A Christian probability-hope concerning progress *is* open to such revision.

We have considered the New Testament vision of the End and we have introduced an important contrast between certainty-hope and probability-hope which will also be used later. Now we ask, 'Is there any New Testament hope concerning progress?'

The early Christians hoped that the Gospel would not only be preached to men in all nations but also accepted by men in all nations. They mistakenly thought that the End was *temporally* near, but they followed Paul in believing that it would be delayed until 'the fullness of the Gentiles be come in' (Rom. 11. 25). This conviction concerning progress in the evangelization of mankind provided a basis for the Christian missionary enterprise.

The progress of the Gospel meant that more men began to live 'in Christ', receiving not only *forgiveness* of sins and a *hope* with which to face death and the future but also, and primarily, a *new power to love*. The hidden mystery of life in Christ was expressed in a new mode of life. As Emil Brunner says, 'Where Christ reigns in the heart, a change takes place, not only in the hidden depths but also in outward conduct . . . From the centre of innermost personal renewal, there comes to pass that slow and secret revolution which really alters conditions because first of all men themselves have been changed, there arise new manners, new law, a new shaping of life, new art, new literature, new culture . . . Even in the outward husk of human life, the state, there comes to be much that is new' (*Eternal Hope,* London, 1954, p. 68).

The early Christians, however, did not hope or try to influence culture and the state. Their hope was not that Christian influence would gradually reform and transform society, but that more men would begin to live in Christ, more individuals would join the Christian fellowship which already participates in the End. There were two reasons for this restricted focus of hope: the belief that the End would come very soon, so that long-range expectations were irrelevant, and the lack of influence or power to affect the affairs of society.

Christians today live in a very different situation, in which the question of possible progress for human society is inescapable. The situation is different in three respects:

First, although Christians today resemble the early Christians in not knowing the date of the End, they differ in that they have no strong expectation that it will come soon. The End might come in 2000 AD; but it also might come in 2,000,000 AD.

Second, Christians in many countries today have enough political power to affect society considerably. (This is not true in Communist countries, where the New Testament focus of hope is correspondingly more appropriate.)

Third, and most important, Christians today share with other men a development of natural science and social science which enables men to produce deliberate and radical changes not only in nature but also in society. The possibilities of purposive human control over both nature and society have increased enormously. Today, Christians can hope to affect society not only by personal influence on other individuals (like second century Christians) and not only by personal political activity (like Christian princes), but in a new way: by joining with other men of good will in social legislation, economic planning, educational reforms and other applications of modern science. These change society so that *people* are changed. Modern science provides a new basis of hope, not only for Communists, but also for many scientifically-minded men who reject the Marxist-Leninist version of that hope. Modern science confronts Christians with an inescapable issue.

Where do Christians today stand concerning this issue? The truth of the matter is that Christians do not agree. Some Christians reject all hope for progress in human society. Others do not, maintaining a probability-hope which varies in degree of expectation. The Christian pessimists (whose 'pessimism' may be joined with an optimistic certainty-hope concerning the *End*) set forth three kinds of objection: theological, philosophical and historical. In each case, the Christian optimists provide counter-arguments. What follows is an attempt to illustrate these unresolved issues in Christian thought.

Theological Issues

Can sin be overcome?

No: Sin is universal in mankind; the tendency towards proud self-assertion against God is part of human nature; it is innate in every individual who is born into the world. Moreover, the power of sin is not overcome even in converted Christians, who are still forgiven sinners, not second Christs.

Yes: Surely Christians believe that sin *can* be overcome by God in those who respond to his work in Christ; surely Christians can learn to *love*; surely Christians can grow in *grace*.

Is history a repetitious see-saw?

Yes: The affairs of nations and empires will always follow the same pattern as they did in Old Testament times: a see-saw between progress (salvation) and regress (judgment).

No: The Resurrection has begun a new Age, the reign of Christ, which can gradually displace the see-saw pattern of the earlier Age.

Does God use impersonal power?

No: God works only in a personal way, using love and persuasion to influence individuals and small fellowships. He does not work through impersonal power-structures, politics or legislation or applications of social science.

Yes: God uses unwilling instruments to achieve his purposes, and he acts in and through the power-structures and impersonal relations and social planning of men. Hence cumulative social progress is possible.

Is belief in progress atheistic?

Yes: Belief in progress is belief in an immanent power within nature and history which ensures progress. It is an alternative to belief in God.

No: Some belief in progress *is* atheistic, for example that of Communists or nineteenth century free-enterprisers. But Christians have a probability-hope in progress, not a faith in it, and their hope includes their faith in God.

Philosophical Issue

Is moral progress possible in history?

No: Moral freedom means that the individual does not depend on his natural or social environment, but can rise above it. Moral worth consists in the extent to which he does rise above it. Hence freedom and moral worth are independent of changes in society. Hence each generation of men is in exactly the same position in relation to possible moral achievement. Hence there can be no historical progress in morality.

Yes: Moral freedom is a power of the individual which does depend on his environment very considerably, especially on the influence of other persons who may strengthen or weaken this freedom. 'We are members one of another, even in moral experience' (D. D. Williams). Furthermore, moral worth depends not only on how high a man rises above his environment but also on his intrinsic worth. For example, John Wesley may perhaps have been no 'better' than King David in rising above his environment, but he was surely in many ways a 'better' man.

Historical Issues

Is technological progress important?

No: It is true that there has been considerable progress in technology since the time of Jesus, but this progress is spiritually irrelevant. Furthermore, it has merely given men power to do large-scale evil as well as large-scale good.

Yes: Technological advance has already freed millions of people from joyless drudgery and irremediable suffering, which has been the life of most men during history. There is a reasonable hope that this can be extended to millions more. Christian 'materialism' cannot under-rate the importance of this. God has appointed man to rule over nature.

Has there been social progress?

No: The institutions of society have changed since the time of Jesus, and some of the changes have been for the better. But each advance in political or social organization brings new problems of organization which are always beyond the ability of men to cope with at the time. Man moves from crisis to crisis. Recently Germany produced Nazism, and now we all live under the threat of nuclear annihilation. All in all, most of mankind are no better off than most of mankind were 1900 years ago.

Yes: Perhaps the last claim is true, but we think not. Even if it were true, the fact remains that some societies today are better for all their inhabitants than *any* societies which existed in the past. There is a reasonable hope that this progress can spread eventually to other societies and increase. Modern social science gives men tools for improving society in a rational way.

Has the Church progressed?

No: Since the time of Jesus the Church has contributed to society a mixture of good and evil which cancel each other out. The Church has been as prone to sin as any other group, and God has had to purge it and punish it many times. Recently, the rise of Communism has been God's judgment on a callous and conformist Church. Indeed, much of the progress in the West towards economic justice, religious toleration and political freedom has occurred in spite of the Church, not because of it. Reformers whom we now applaud, whether they were Christian or atheist, were usually opposed by the Church in their day.

Yes: If the historical balance-sheet of the Church includes its moral and spiritual influence on millions of individuals in their daily lives, the good exceeds the bad, and there *has* been progress. It is true that the Church is prone to sin, but it has been specially open to reform and renewal, and has often been the conscience of the State. It is true that God often by-passes the Church to use other instruments to achieve his purpose; but although this is humbling for the Church it provides an additional basis for a hope of progress.

Has there been missionary progress?

No: The mission of the Church in the world has been more of a failure than a success. Christianity has indeed spread around the world, but it has suffered major setbacks at the hands of Islam and Communism, it has failed to displace Hinduism and Buddhism, and in the West it has been weakened internally by secularism. In few countries today is Christianity a dominant influence.

Yes: It is true that the Church may not have much direct social and political power today, but that is no measure of failure. The seed of the gospel has been sown in every land. It has exercised a revolutionary and transforming effect on Hindu and Buddhist cultures. It still is an enormous power for good in the secularized West.

> The greatest missionary successes of the Gospel are hidden and undramatic, like the leaven in the dough or the seed growing secretly.

We have presented a few of the issues which are debated today among Christians. At one extreme, some Christian pessimists have what might be called a confident 'probability-*despair*': things are going to get worse and worse. At the other extreme, there are Christian optimists who have a confident probability-hope for a splendid human future—not the End, but a harmonious society in which many men will have the Christ-likeness of St Francis and in which nature will be radically changed by these same men, exercising Christian stewardship in the use of advancing scientific knowledge.

Most Christians (wisely, in our opinion) avoid either extreme pessimism or extreme optimism. But whatever their hopes concerning progress, Christians have three fundamentals in common:

First, their ultimate hope, which gives meaning and purpose to their lives, is not focused on future society at all, but on Christ. This Christian hope frees them from either a crippling pessimism or a naïve optimism, enabling them to deal concretely with human problems in the *present*.

Second, their expression of Christian love in modern society includes an attempt to improve society (or at least to prevent it from getting worse). Individual influence on other persons is not enough, though it is still central.

Third, their hope concerning the future, even at its most optimistic is a *probability*-hope concerning an objective which is of limited value in comparison with the End. So Christians are not willing to sacrifice the happiness and the moral integrity of present generations for the sake of generations in the distant future.

These three fundamentals are also shared by Christians whose interpretation of the End has not been considered here. Some Christians interpret biblical language concerning the End in the same way as most Christians today interpret the biblical story of Adam and Eve, or the biblical references to

God's location way up in the sky; that is, they interpret it as symbolic imagery. Just as spatial imagery is used to express the 'distance' between every man and God, and just as the Eden story is used to express the rebellion of every man against God, so the temporal images of an End or Last Day are used to express the ultimate divine context for every human decision and action. This means that 2000 AD will not be any 'nearer' to the 'End' than 1964 AD is. The certainty-hope in an End is a way of expressing our certainty-hope in Christ *now*. This certainty-hope is compatible with a Christian optimism or a Christian pessimism concerning the future progress of humanity.

The common core of Christian conviction is well expressed in these words of John Baillie:

'The Christian's attitude to civilization must be a double one. He must strive to bring it as near to the Christian ideal of life in community as is possible in a world of sinful men, but he must never give it his absolute approval or unconditional loyalty; he must place in it only such a strictly qualified hope as would, even if it were to suffer complete shipwreck, leave his ultimate hope as securely anchored as before' (*What is Christian Civilization?*, Oxford, 1945, p. 56).

MORALITY

(See also chapters 2 and 3)

(i) *The essentials of Christian morality.*

We have seen that Christian morality is not a matter of bringing some utopian system or other into being but of consciously participating in God's historical activity in Jesus Christ which is evident to the eyes of faith.

The Christian life is a life of faith, hope and love: faith in forgiveness, hope in the End, and love of the neighbour. It is a response to God's act of forgiveness, resurrection and love in Jesus Christ. It is a participation in the risen life of Jesus Christ within the Church, which makes man a 'co-worker' with God.

Christian morality has one simple criterion: obedience to God's will.

The criterion is simple, but its application is complex. The Christian has no infallible way of knowing God's will in each particular situation of moral decision. He first examines the facts of the situation, and then he makes his moral decision in relation to four guides:

Scripture, especially the teaching of Jesus,
Church teaching,
Conscience and the moral judgment of others,
Prayer.

These guides do not answer every moral question like the answers at the back of a quiz-book. They provide the Christian context for moral reflection and moral decision. Sometimes the will of God seems obvious, and the problem is not 'What ought I to do?', but 'Have I the moral strength to do it?' Sometimes, however, the will of God is not obvious: the Christian is profoundly perplexed concerning what to do, for the guides offer conflicting counsel or no counsel.

In such situations the Christian's trust in justification by *grace* is specially important. A Christian realizes that his ultimate status does not depend on his moral perfection but on God's gracious acceptance of him. His task is not to earn merit but to respond to grace. So a Christian need not try to justify himself by claiming a false certainty or infallibility for his moral judgments. His responsibility is simply to try his best to choose and to do what is right. He is justified by grace, not by works. He lives by faith in God's forgiveness.

The Christian ethic is an ethic of love. The Christian responds to God's love by sharing in it. This love, as revealed in Jesus Christ, is an undeviating and active goodwill towards each and every man. It is a spirit or attitude or motive which is focused on the material and spiritual well-being of others.

The Christian ethic is thus focused on a *motive* which is concerned with *consequences*. We do not truly love someone unless we are concerned about the consequences of our actions in relation to him. Sometimes we are in direct personal contact with a man, our immediate neighbour. Then the spirit of our action makes a difference to him, altering the consequences: God may even use us to reveal himself to him. Often, however, our actions affect people whom we do not know and who do not know us, and to whom we are related only through the impersonal power-structures of society. Then the consequences to these people are still important; concern for justice to them is an expression of Christian love. And although the spirit of the action may not affect the consequences for these people, the spirit is important in the eyes of God. For in relation to the *End*, what matters is the spirit or motive: 'Your labour is not in vain, *in the Lord*' (1 Cor. 15.58).

Christian love *for* the neighbour has for its fundamental goal Christian love *by* the neighbour—that is, his responding to the love of God by sharing in it. But the content of Christian love is a concern for his total well-being: food and friends, shelter and work, health and happiness, security and freedom. This concern is sometimes expressed in intimate personal fellowship and sometimes in remote economic legislation. The Christian should choose the most effective means to achieve the end.

The New Testament provides considerable guidance for Christians in their personal relations to immediate neighbours and to fellow Christians. For example, the Sermon on the Mount sets forth non-resistance to personal injury, and St Paul's description of love in I Corinthians sets forth the attitudes which promote Christian unity. The New Testament, however, provides little guidance for modern Christians who have power and responsibility in society. How is a Christian to deal with injuries done to others? How is a Christian to express his concern for the unemployed?

In this study booklet we are not trying to cover the whole of Christian morality. The central area of individual and Church-fellowship morality has not been discussed in detail.

However, in chapter 3 we have already tried to state

some general principles for Christian action in economic life. In this section we shall try to do the same for political life, insofar as it can be distinguished from economic life.

(ii) *Christian principles for political action*

(I) *Political Humility* (God is judge) All political systems and political groups and political causes come under the judgment of God.

The fundamental sin in politics is idolatry, the claim that God is automatically on *our* side. This claim is really a way of turning 'our side' into a *god*.

The fact that a political opponent is an atheist or that he has different convictions concerning God is not a good reason for identifying our own cause absolutely with the will of God.

The Christian in politics as in personal life lives by the forgiveness of God, having faith in it, and acknowledging his need of it.

(II) *Political Realism* (All men are prone to sin) Human sin gives rise to a fundamental political problem which men must face, in one form or another, in *every* society. As Reinhold Niebuhr has pointed out, 'social co-operation on a large scale requires a measure of coercion'. Coercive power is never spread out equally among men; some men have more than others. Those who have most are tempted to use it to further their own interests rather than those of other people. Few can resist this temptation. The result is injustice. The problem which must be faced is this:

'to place the most effective possible inner moral and external social checks in order that the perennial tendencies towards injustice in society may be retarded' (R. Niebuhr, in *Christianity and the Social Revolution*, ed. Lewis, pp. 464-5).

The most realistic way to tackle this problem is political (and economic) democracy. Since no group can be trusted with power over those who have no chance to criticize it or to control it, all government which is allegedly *for* the people must be checked by a large measure of government *by* the people. The Assembly of the World Council of Churches at Evanston set forth four requirements for political institutions:

'1. Every person should be protected against arbitrary arrest or other interference with elementary human rights.
2. Every person should have the right to express his religious, moral and political convictions. This is especially important for those who belong to minorities.
3. Channels of political action must be developed by which the people can without recourse to violence change their governments.
4. Forms of association within society which have their own foundations and principles should be respected, and not controlled in their inner life by the state. Churches, families, and universities are dissimilar examples of this non-political type of association.'

Political realism does not imply that full-scale democracy can be achieved overnight in a country which has scarcely known it. In such countries a Communist tyranny may be the only realistic alternative to the tyranny which exists. But where a large measure of democracy has been achieved by the gradual development of moral and social checks on power, the loss of such democracy is a great tragedy. And even where a strong central government is needed for rapid industrialization and radical changes in the relations of production —needed if the masses are to have the necessities of life—the need for checks on power should be acknowledged.

(III) *Political Responsibility* (God loves all men) Christian love for the neighbour is expressed not only by direct personal help but also by indirect political action. The latter has become more important for Christians than it used to be:

'That which on the whole distinguishes the most recent Christian thinking from the attitudes of the great Churches in the past is the conviction that Christian responsibility for society includes a responsibility for radical criticism of the existing order. This has led to organized efforts—usually taking political forms—to change the structures of society so that they may be more favourable to justice and to fraternal relations among men.'

'People who have been neglected and exploited in the past have . . . acquired a voice so that they could say how the world appeared to them. They have been able to talk back to those who had kept to themselves the privilege and the power. They have been able to speak to the conscience of the Church and to win much support for their aspirations. They have been able to show how hollow many of the expressions of Christian love were, when they took a paternalistic form, and raised no question concerning the *power* of those at the top, which *enabled* them to do good things for others.'

'Intelligent love for the neighbour must be concerned about the effect of economic institutions and policies upon persons. When it becomes apparent that any persons are hungry or thirsty or strangers or naked or sick or in prison as a result of conditions which can be brought to an end by changing economic institutions or by corporate action of any kind, the Christian must translate the injunctions of the Gospel into such action' (John Bennett, *The Christian as Citizen,* pp. 15-18).

Christian responsibility in political life involves Christians in compromises. 'There are situations in which those who do not do what may be necessary to prevent some great evil, such as aggression that brings with it political and cultural tyranny, share responsibility for that evil. If they do act to prevent it, they may in their methods be involved in compromise, but any alternative that is available may be morally worse. Those who have not faced this kind of decision do not realize the depth of evil and tragedy in human life' (J. Bennett, *Christianity and Communism Today,* p. 92).

Some Christians are tempted to 'contract out' of the State and politics, trying to remain untainted by the evils of society. But such an action itself has political consequences for which the Christian is responsible. The individual Christian, like other individuals, has responsibilities to society.

Society, however, has responsibilities to the individual, Christians have two basic reasons for insisting on this:

'The status of the individual person depends upon the love of God. There are many reasons why persons of obvious dignity and worth should be respected, but these reasons break down when persons lose their obvious dignity and worth. They may lose their status in this sense when they seem morally lost or when they become shiftless non-producers or when they become enemies or opponents of our nation or class or cause. But the Christian gospel stands or falls with the faith in the aggressive love of God for those who do not deserve it on any human basis.'

'The individual person is the ultimate unit of moral and religious decision. No one else can repent for him. No one else can respond in faith to the truth in his place. No one else can assume his moral responsibility. No external authority can create in him conscience or moral insight or that inner awareness of what is good on which his judgments depend . . . Christians must seek the kind of spiritual freedom . . . in which it is externally possible for the truth to be accepted or rejected' (*Christianity and Communism Today,* pp. 102-3).

(IV) *Political Morality* (God judges the heart) We have seen that Christians have a responsibility to find political means whereby people in need can be helped, and we have seen that Christians are responsible for failure to use these means. But although Christian political morality does not rule out moral compromises, it does impose *limits* on the means which can be used.

(a) *Some actions are intrinsically wrong,* even if the consequences are in many ways beneficial. During the last war, for example, a commission of American theologians said this:

'All of us agree that in war some practices cannot be regarded by the Church as justifiable: the killing of prisoners, of hostages, or of refugees to lessen military handicaps or to gain military advantages; the torture of prisoners or of hostages to gain military information, however vital; the massacre of civilian populations' (Quoted by J. Bennett, *C. and C.T.*, p. 95).

(b) *Some attitudes are intrinsically wrong,* even if the consequences of actions which express these attitudes are in many ways beneficial. Hatred of the enemy of one's nation or class is wrong, for it impedes subsequent *reconciliation* when victory is achieved. Christian love includes love of the enemy. When this love is real, it shows itself in action wherever such action is possible—for example in the treatment of prisoners of war or in personal help to a political opponent who is in need. Moreover, Christian love rejects the deliberate cultivation of hatred towards another race, class or nation.

(c) Christians insist that the consequences of political action include its *moral consequences for the agents.* If the means involve the agents in a deliberate inflicting of suffering on masses of people, the total situation is worse than that in a society in which similar suffering occurs as the unintended product of the economic system. Christians have no formula for weighing the importance of these moral consequences in relation to other consequences, and Christians cannot escape involvement in moral compromise; but a universal *policy* of using some men *merely* as means to an end is clearly un-Christian.

(d) The fundamental goal in love of the neighbour is *love by the neighbour.* This is what will be preserved in the *End.* All other goals are subordinate. This subordination imposes limits on the political means which can be employed by Christians.

(iii) *The state and revolution*

In the modern world many Christians have to decide whether or not to participate in violent revolution. Often the issue arises because of Communism. In one country, a Christian may wonder whether to support a revolution against a Communist government. In another country, a Christian may wonder whether to support a Communist-led revolution against a non-Communist government.

Like war, the violent overthrow of public order is in most cases an almost unmitigated evil. But unless a Christian is a pacifist, he has to face the question of possible participation not only in war but also, perhaps, in revolution. There are situations in which Christians have to decide whether or not to use violence against tyranny.

The New Testament provides little guidance in such situations. No political action by Christian citizens was seriously considered by the New Testament writers; Christians were a helpless minority, and the End was believed to be imminent. In Romans 13.1 we read the injunction, 'Let every person be subject to the governing authorities'; but this does not guide the Christian citizen of a modern democratic state insofar as *he* is one of the governing authorities (government *by* the people). In Romans 13.1-3 we read that the existing authorities have been instituted by God as his servants and are not to be resisted; and we read that they are a terror to bad conduct and not to good conduct. In Revelation 13.7, however, the state is pictured as a blasphemous beast which makes war on the saints. The general conclusion seems to be this: The state as such is an institution which comes under God's providential care and authority, but one's attitude to each particular state must depend on what sort of a state it is.

The New Testament does not consider the possibility of Christian participation in a 'just revolution', and it does not consider the possibility of Christian participation in a 'just war'. But the possibility of two forms of *non*-violent resistance to the state is clearly indicated.

Spiritual resistance to the state is an inner rejection of any claim to total and unconditional obedience. It is the refusal to submit inwardly to any absolute state authority or ideology. This may involve external submission, but the submission is rendered to *God*, from whom all power and authority is ultimately derived. As Jesus said to Pilate, 'You would have no power over me unless it had been given you from above' (John 19.11).

Civil disobedience is the refusal to obey a particular law or command of the state. The early Christians refused to stop preaching the Gospel or to begin worshipping Caesar. The words of Peter and the apostles are typical: 'We must obey God rather than men' (Acts 5.29). In recent times also, Christians have refused to obey state commands which are contrary to conscience—for example, bearing false witness in a political trial.

Concerning political change, however, the New Testament provides no clear teaching. Indeed, New Testament passages concerning submission to God-given authorities have been used by rulers in every century to *prevent* political change. Nor has subsequent Christian thought provided theology of the 'just revolution' comparable to the traditional theology of the 'just war'. The beginnings of such a theology, however, can be found in sixteenth and seventeenth century Calvinism, which became involved in various bourgeois revolutions against feudal governments. And in recent times, various Christian thinkers have wrestled with the problem.

The criteria for a just revolution can best be derived from those which earlier Christian theology developed for a just war. Non-pacifist Christians have held that, in order to be considered just, a war must satisfy the following conditions:

'1. It must be declared by the public authority: no private war.
2. It must be intended to repel an enemy's attack: no aggressive war.
3. A good result must be possible, and proportionate to the sacrifice involved: no hopeless or disproportionate war.
4. The force used must be proportionate to the enemy's attack: no unlimited war.
5. Non-combatants must be spared with reasonable discrimination: no war of obliteration.'

(Summarized by D. L. Edwards, *Withdrawing from the Brink in 1963,* SCM 1963, p. 17.)

Modern nuclear weapons have raised new issues concerning the 'just war' doctrine. Some Christian theologians claim that the doctrine is no longer applicable; others disagree. Moreover, new ethical problems are raised concerning the *threat* of war, as distinct from war itself: Is it permissible to use the threat of civilian massacre as a deterrent?

We cannot consider these issues here. What we wish to suggest is that the criteria for a just war are applicable, with appropriate changes, in the case of modern revolutions:

1. *Public.* A just revolution must be organized by a group which has at least the implicit support of a majority of the population and which has a reasonable hope of replacing the existing public authority by another and better one. No private revolutionary violence is justifiable.
2. *Defensive.* A revolution is warranted only if non-violent means of change (by political organization or by non-violent demonstrations, etc.) have been repressed by the government, which has thus committed aggression against the mass of the people.
3. *Successful.* The revolution must have a reasonable prospect of success. That is, not only must victory over the existing government be highly probable, but this new government must be so much better that the improvement is proportionate to the sacrifice which a revolution involves.
4. *Limited.* No unlimited revolution is warranted. That is, the success of the revolution is not an end which justifies the use of *all* means which are effective. The revolution is not to be regarded as a crusade or holy war.
5. *Merciful.* The obliteration of all who support the existing regime is not a legitimate objective. Only the achievement of victory and the protection of the new government are legitimate objectives. Also, non-combatants must be spared with reasonable discrimination.

These criteria do not provide a simple formula for Christian decision, but they do indicate some essentials which should be considered if Christian decision is to be responsible. Christian pacifists of course have the right to dissent from the 'just revolution' as they dissent from the 'just war'.

Reinhold Niebuhr once made the ironic comment that 'the modern Church always has more pacifistic scruples against the use of force by a political group which is protesting against social injustice than against the violence of the State when it engages other nations in combat' (*Christianity and the Social*

Revolution, ed. Lewis, p. 453).[3] On the other hand, the traditional Christian stress on the dangers of anarchy and on the value of continuity or 'legitimacy' is extremely relevant in many restless countries today. Also, the modern methods of non-violent protest which have been developed in India and the southern United States have serious claim to Christian consideration as an alternative to violent revolution, which so rarely is 'just'.

Commentary

Disagreements with Communism

(1) *Evil and its remedy*

Christians must reject the basic Communist conviction concerning moral evil. The decisive cause of moral evil is not private ownership of the means of production. The decisive remedy of moral evil is not social ownership under the leadership of the Party.

Marx remarked somewhere that no particular class can claim to rule without pretending that it does so in the name of the general rights of society. Communists fail to apply this insight to themselves. The Communist Party in a socialist state is a new class, as the Communist heretic Djilas has pointed out. It wields tremendous economic and political power, and it justifies its rule in the old familiar way. J. M. Cameron has summarized the two inter-related delusions of Marxism-Leninism: 'that the ownership of property is the only remaining form of despotic social power; and that,

[3] A notable exception to this is a recent statement by a Working Party of the British Council of Churches: 'Unless we accept the full pacifist position ourselves and reserve no right to use force to defend ourselves against possible totalitarian domination, we have no moral right to deny to non-whites within the Republic of South Africa the right to resistance by force' (*The Future of South Africa,* SCM Press, 1965, pp. 55-6). The Working Party did not recommend, however, that this right be exercised at the present time. (D. E)

whereas *before* the revolution men are ruled by vast impersonal forces, *after* the revolution men will be ruled by reason and good will' (*Scrutiny of Marxism*, p. 39).

Christians differ in their hopes or fears concerning the results of Communist revolution and rule. Some Christians believe that, in their particular country, it may mean a better regime. But Christians cannot agree that it is a panacea. There are two reasons for this. First, Christians believe that sin is the decisive cause of moral evil and that the Gospel is the divine remedy. Sin cannot be overcome by men apart from God, for sin *consists* in being apart from God; no purely human remedy can cure this alienation from God which is the root of moral evil. Second, Christians, along with many non-Christian opponents of Communism, believe that there are many different causes of moral evil, and many different ways of reducing it; economic injustice and economic reform are only a *part* of human life.

The basic Communist conviction generates a false hope and a false morality. Communists believe that their participation in the 'revolutionary process of society which is taking place before our very eyes' is participation in an inexorable dialectical process which is at work in history, and will eventually solve the essential problems of human life. Hence their commitment to the process, and to the Party which knows and spear-heads the process, is total and absolute. It is a *religious* kind of commitment. It is an idolatrous religious commitment, for history becomes a substitute for God.

Communist theory is an example of religious theory at its worst. Communist theory promotes religious pride, fanaticism and utopianism. Christians and other religious people are always in danger of religious pride, fanaticism and utopianism in their *practice*; but Christian teaching provides a constant rebuke to these religious evils. Communist theory, however, reinforces these evils in Communist practice.

Christians have no reason to feel smug as they point out these radical defects in Communist teaching, for *in practice* Christians have often fallen into the same errors.

(2) *Religious pride*

The Communist assurance that 'history is on our side' is like the smug religious assurance of early Israel when the prophet Amos challenged it; it is like the crusading pride of Christendom when it has claimed to *be* the Kingdom of God. Communist self-righteousness and ruthlessness are not checked by any sense of being under judgment, for their 'god'—history—does not judge them. The only verdict is the verdict of history, and Communists claim to know that verdict already.

No one can master the true God, but Communists believe that they can master history. Moreover, Communists think that they are the instruments of history in destroying the decisive cause of moral evil; so any means seems to be justified if it contributes to their political success.

Christians hold that men are God's *stewards over nature*. But Christians deny that any group can set itself up as *custodians of the historical future*. History differs from nature. It cannot be mastered in the same way as nature, and men ought not to try to master it in the same way as nature. There are three reasons for this:

(i) *Moral*. Men are not things. There are moral limitations on the deliberate manipulation of persons. The Communist parallel between freedom over nature and freedom over society is immoral in so far as it involves 'social engineering'; individual persons are used as cogs in the machinery of historical 'progress'.

(ii) *Scientific*. Men are not things. There are scientific limitations on historical prediction. These limitations may decrease, and Christians should not oppose attempts to increase the predictive powers of social science. The Communist certainty-hope, however, is not acknowledged as the religious faith which it is; it is falsely represented as a piece of science. Scientific predictions can at best only claim a very high degree of probability, never absolute certainty.

(iii) *Biblical*. Men are not gods. Those who claim to master history are pretending to be gods. As Herbert Butterfield has said, 'The hardest strokes of heaven fall in history upon those who imagine that they can control things in a sovereign manner . . . playing Providence not only for themselves but for the far future' (*Christianity and History*, p. 137).

Communist theory maintains that history is on their side, and Communist 'history' is a god. Whenever Christians who have joined in a political or religious cause against others have cried, 'God is on our side', they have also been involved in the same sort of pride. Christian theology, however, warns men that this is a sin, not a virtue.

(3) *Religious fanaticism*

Christians must reject the totalitarian fanaticism of Communist theory.

It is true that a genuine Christian faith means that a Christian spirit will pervade *all* a man's activities, so that a Christian commitment is a total commitment. But Christian faith regards fanaticism as a dangerous evil.

The religious fanatic subordinates all *morality* to a particular cause, movement or group.

The religious fanatic subordinates all *truth* to a particular cause, movement or group.

The religious fanatic subordinates all *individuals* to a particular cause, movement or group.

Communist theory promotes religious fanaticism in each of these three ways. Indeed, it holds that its most dangerous ideological enemies are 'idealism' concerning morals, 'objectivism' concerning truth, and 'liberalism' concerning individuals.(See pages 96-7.) Christians must reject this Communist fanaticism:

(i) *Morality*. Christians are not committed to a philosophy of moral 'idealism' which is concerned only with human motives or with abstract moral ideas and laws. Christians agree with Communists that the consequences of an action are extremely important. But Christians hold that motives matter, and that there are moral limits on what can be done for the Communist cause or for any particular human cause. Christians insist that political responsibility is qualified by political morality. (See pages 123-4.)

(ii) *Truth.* Christians are not committed to a philosophical theory of 'objectivism' in which all truth is supposedly independent of ideological viewpoint. Christians agree that in politics and morality there is no 'neutral' position from which 'objective' interpretations and appraisals can be made. Nevertheless Christians believe that there is a core of *fact* in every situation, which men should respect. It is morally disastrous if deliberate lying becomes a matter of policy, supposedly justified on the ground that it promotes the Communist cause and is thereby 'true'. (Communist theory of truth promotes such lying, although Communists will deny that it *is* lying.) Furthermore, Christians should uphold the autonomy of science. There is no 'Christian physics', just as there is no 'Communist physics'—or ought not to be. One need not be a Christian (or a Communist) in order to discover truth, and one may be a Christian (or a Communist) and be in gross error. Christian truth is understood and confirmed in relation to Christian practice; but *other* kinds of truth do not necessarily depend on Christian practice.

(iii) *Individuals.* Christians are not committed to a philosophical theory of 'liberalism' in which the individual has no responsibilities to society and in which his freedom from government interference is all that matters. But Christians must reject the Communist emphasis on *group* freedom and on freedom as *control over society*, for this means the mastery of individuals by the group or its leaders. The responsibilities of society to the individual are responsibilities for today; visions of individual freedom in a classless society are no substitute. Moreover, Communist teaching concerning political opponents is contrary to Christian convictions concerning the dignity of all men in the eyes of God. Communist theory is opposed to any love for political enemies. The only thing to do to opponents is to convert them or remove them. This is religious fanaticism at its worst.

Communists point out that Christians have sometimes been fanatical in the assertion of their cause, subordinating all morality, truth and individual freedom to its success. Christian religious persecutions have sometimes warranted this charge, and so has Christian conduct in war. But Christian faith, rightly understood, is firmly opposed to fanaticism. Communist faith, rightly understood, *is* fanatical.

(4) *Religious utopianism*

Communists' criticisms of religion have been focused on various utopian errors:

(i) the unrealistic idealism which foolishly hopes to change society merely by changing human thinking.

(ii) the false fantasies concerning heaven and God which cheat men of their worth and value by projecting it into a future heaven or into an ideal being called 'God'.

(iii) the opiate of the people, a hope for a future heaven which will provide the satisfaction denied to them in the present.

These criticisms of bad religion are perceptive. But Communist theory is open to the same criticisms:

(i) The Communist foolishly hopes that changes in the ideas of men (education in Marxism-Leninism) will bring about the changes in men which are required for the transition from socialism to communism. Communists are unrealistic idealists in their failure to recognize the need for institutional checks on economic power. Preaching Marxism-Leninism to a wealthy and powerful Communist bureaucrat is like preaching benevolence to a nineteenth century industrialist: it is not enough.

(ii) The Communist vision of a classless society in the future cheats men today of their full worth and value, since only future generations can enjoy real life. Communists project all real history, real morality and real individual freedom into the future. This is worse than the false other-worldliness which Communists rightly denounce when it occurs among Christians, for even if it is supposed that a Christian pilgrim can only enjoy real life after death, this is a possibility for those on earth today. Communist utopianism, however, can assure a real human existence only to future generations. It is true that the 1961 Russian Programme promises communism to this generation of Russians, but even if this promise were to be fulfilled, previous generations will have been merely manure for the harvest. In the Christian 'End', all generations will participate; this is part of what is meant by the 'general resurrection'.

(iii) Communist talk about the classless society, especially talk about its freedom and moral perfections, is an opiate which induces resignation in the masses, preventing counter-revolution. Communist slogans such as 'public self-government will replace the state' work like a drug, enabling unhappy men to escape from the miseries of state oppression in this life by hoping for a better one in the future. Even if some of the Communist hopes are not illusory—for example, the hope of expanding production—they are used as substitutes for present satisfaction, just like the non-illusory hopes of Christians whose religion has become too other-worldly.

Once again, Christian disagreements with Communist theory should not be an occasion for smugness, but rather for reflection concerning Christian failure in practice. Christian utopianism is contrary to Christian teaching, but it is not uncommon. (Moreover, if it is true that Christian practice often falls short of Christian theory, it is also true that Communist practice is sometimes not as bad as Communist theory. Religious pride, fanaticism and utopianism in Russian Communism seem to be moderating, and Russian theory is gradually being revised accordingly—provoking the wrath of Communist revolutionaries elsewhere.[4])

(5) *Death*

The early Marx thought that although the individual man

[4] That is, Chinese or pro-Chinese Communists. The Russian revision of Communist theory should be compared with that of Adam Schaff (p. 98, n. 2), which is more radical. Christians should welcome these trends towards less religious fanaticism and utopianism. Nevertheless, the change should not be exaggerated. The revised Marxism-Leninism may be slightly more humane, but it could surely afford to be! It is still a long way from Christian 'humanism'. Nor does the decrease in ideological rigidity necessarily mean an increased tolerance towards religion. In Russia it has been accompanied by a stepped-up campaign against the Church. (D. E.)

dies and only the human species continues, this merely *seems* to be a harsh victory of the species over the individual. Marxism-Leninism has continued to refrain from taking death seriously, as a tragedy. Alexander Miller points out that this makes for a failure in reverence for human life 'and so for a general failure in compassion and in consideration for individuals . . . Regard for human life goes down the drain with every other kind of obligation except that to the Party. In fact, in the exigencies of the revolutionary struggle it is necessary to make light of death and to sit lightly by human life—one's own and that of one's comrades and friends, and that of one's enemies. The former may have to be sacrificed at any time if Party strategy requires it; and the latter cannot be held of any account if it gets in the way of the programme. The only way to avoid intolerable moral conflict is to "write down" the value of human life' (*The Christian Significance of Karl Marx,* pp. 67-8).

Christians believe that the taking of a human life is an infinitely serious matter. Death itself is a tragic shadow, a 'tearing away', as Gollwitzer said; life is terribly precious. Death is something which humanly speaking, each man faces alone in his loneliness. The Christian assurance that in Christ we are not alone does not mean that death is to be treated lightly. Until death is abolished in the End, each human life stands under its sentence. Even if all the most wonderful dreams of communism were to be fulfilled, the fact of death would remain unchanged. Death would still be the great unknown.

Summary

Charles West sums up many of the Christian disagreements with Communism in a passage which includes a warning against making anti-Communism a religion, and ends with an appeal for a true Christian faith as Christians encounter Communists:

'The world meets Communism as a *tyrannous power*, more thoroughgoing in its claim on human life than any dictatorship in history, because it combines absolute political power with a religious type of claim to authority, infallibility, and destiny. This must be understood against the background of its appeal as a revolutionary force. The quality of its tyranny and the intensity of its claim come from its pretension to be *the* expression of the revolution of our time, and its fulfilment.'

'This same pretension gives a total quality, an absolute intensity, to the experience of those who have suffered under this tyranny or have broken with its hold on their allegiance . . . The Christian theologian stands before the victim and fugitive of Communism as one who must deny him the very thing he wants most of all—another absolute human authority, another ideology, membership in another conquering movement. For precisely this desire is the sickness of his resistance of Communism.'

'The Christian resists the total claims of Communist power and ideology . . . but this prior obedience to Christ is a response to reigning reality, not the promotion of a cause. The Christian resists as the witness to Christ the reconciler, as one who points the Communist to the reality beyond his distortions of truth and breaches of justice, who is a personal Lord, and who forgives and saves, and thus commands. The Christian resists for the sake of the tyrant as well as for the sake of his victim . . . He resists within the framework of God's act of reconciliation, and as witness to it; as one for whom the friend-foe antithesis is no longer the dominant factor, and as one for whom total powers and ideologies are no longer necessary' (*Communism and the Theologians*, pp. 334-7).

Agreements with Communism

(1) *Communist criticisms of Christian religion*

We have seen that the religious excess which Communist theory promotes is an excess into which Christian practice may fall. Communist criticisms of this excess (pride, fanaticism, utopianism) are often true. Where this is so, it must be acknowledged. God is not interested in hearing from us about Communist sins. As Johannes Hamel said, 'We cannot wash ourselves clean with the evil of others'. Communist criticism may express the judgment of God on Christians.

(2) *Communist emphases*

All Christians should accept some of the general emphases in Marxist-Leninist thought, without necessarily accepting it in detail. (Some Christians may, of course, accept much of the detail as well.) For instance:

History matters. The Christian hope is not an escape from history but a hope *for* history.

Technology matters. Advances in man's control of nature can mean a reduction of human suffering and a fulfilment of man's task as God's steward.

Progress matters. Whether or not progress is likely, it is worth striving for.

Economics matters. Communism is not a panacea, but its insistence on the importance of economic factors in human life cannot be ignored.

Christian Options

Some Christians accept the general outlines of Marxism-Leninism as a theory of history, while rejecting its religious pretensions and subordinating it to a Christian view of history. Alexander Miller's position is representative.

Other Christians reject the general outlines of Marxism-Leninism as a theory of history, reject its religious pretensions, and set forth a Christian view of history which is in conflict with it. Emil Brunner's position is representative.

Many other Christians have views which lie somewhere between Miller and Brunner. A great many different views are possible.

We shall conclude with two quotations for consideration, one from Miller and the other from Brunner.

'Transcending every secular interpretation of history—as, for example, that illuminating interpretation in which primitive society gives way to feudalism and feudalism to capitalism—there is a world view of which the Incarnation is the centre and the Gospel gives the meaning. That pattern remains the ground-plan of the historic process, however much it may be blurred by church-apostasy, or overlaid by humanly-momentous events in the secular world. To accept it and take it seriously means that, in our contemporary world, for example, we shall allow ourselves to be governed not only by the fact that we live in the twilight of capitalism and the socialist-fascist struggle for power, but by the fact that we live in the urgent moment between Christ's Ascension and his coming to judge the world. If we take both with real seriousness, we shall forget neither our political obligation nor our evangelical responsibility. For we shall know that both are laid on us by God' (*The Christian Significance of Karl Marx*, pp. 87-8).

'The Christian faith revolutionizes the idea of revolution in that it perceives the only real revolution to be one which works from within outwards, and all others as mere camouflaged reaction . . . It is an essential law of the working of this revolution from within outwards that it needs time and proceeds as a gradual evolution rather than by fits and starts, and that it lays more emphasis on the motive than on the outward visible effect, that it regards with mistrust, rather than aims at, the outward change which does not of itself follow from the inner transformation. All this makes it an object of suspicion to the revolutionary. The latter aims at immediate changes, and when conditions are ripe easily produces them . . . From the point of view of such a one, the Christian faith, with its hope in what God will accomplish, with its reference to what will come to mankind from the beyond, must appear . . . as a most stubborn reactionary power . . . Lenin was the first to realize that deadly enmity existed between the Christian faith and his communistic revolution. For revolution as he understood it could tolerate no scruples derived from bourgeois morality concerning love of one's neighbour' (*Eternal Hope*, pp. 63-66).

A Personal Postscript

In general, *Communist Faith and Christian Faith* has been well received. Nevertheless, some important criticisms have been made. In this personal postscript, which is entirely my own responsibility, I shall consider five of these criticisms.

1. The first criticism is the most important. Readers have complained that the book does not deal adequately with the current disintegration of Communist ideology. The ideological schism between Russia and China is indicated, but its full implications are ignored. The schism now means that each of the Communist Parties which reject the Chinese position is claiming not only political but also *ideological* autonomy. The Chinese still insist that there ought to be a universal unity in ideology; but such a unity does not exist, and most Communist Parties hold that it *need* not exist. Moreover, the ideological trend in these Parties is towards a more liberal and flexible approach in both internal and external affairs. Christians in the West should realize that the great Communist schism and the trend towards Party autonomy and flexibility have radically changed the international situation. No longer is there a monolithic foe called 'world Communism'. Instead, there is a multitude of national Communist Parties who may become neutrals or even our allies—if realistic diplomacy is employed.

I agree with the substance of this criticism. To some extent it has been met by the personal footnotes which have been added to this edition. Some further discussion, however, is necessary.

Let me suggest an analogy to our present situation. Let us imagine that modern liberal scholarship existed in the sixteenth century, and that a Muslim scholar tried to give an account of the Christian faith in, say, 1535. Not only would he need to describe a great schism between Roman Catholics and Protestants. He would also have to note the beginnings of a disintegration within the Protestant side, a division along both theological and national lines.

Our imaginary Muslim scholar would rightly point out to Muslim strategists the *political* importance of these dramatic changes within the Christian world. But he would mislead his Muslim readers if he implied that a common core of Christian faith no longer existed, or that Christianity no longer provided a rival faith to Islam. Similarly, *Communist Faith and Christian Faith* would mislead Christian readers if it implied that Communism no longer has a common ideological core which is a rival to Christian faith.

The realization that Communism is still such a rival is not a basis for waging a war, even a cold war. Islam is still a rival, but we have learned to co-exist with it, and even to deplore the medieval Crusades against the Muslim world. Both political realism and Christian faith should lead us to the same conclusion concerning Communism. This is not incompatible with the sober realization that a particular Communist nation, like various nations in the past and in the present, may be a threat to the security of others. Such a threat may call for stern defensive or deterrent measures. It does not call for a Crusade.

2. A second criticism of the book is that it has given a boost to the Communist cause. When the largest Protestant church in Canada gives general approval to a report which expresses agreement with some elements in Communist ideology, Communists can quote parts of the report and claim a new respectability. Surely it is irresponsible to help the Communists in this way, providing ammunition for their propaganda. Christians should commit themselves unreservedly to the task of eliminating Communist tyranny from the world.

In reply to this criticism, I must point out what it implies:

that no one should ever say anything good about Communism even if he believes that it is *true*, for the Communists will quote him, and so he will help the Communist cause. The criticism implies, in other words, an anti-Communist Crusade. Such a Crusade, like Communism itself, is opposed to all 'objectivism'; one must only tell the truth if it helps the cause —in this case, not Communism, but anti-Communism. Such a Crusade, like Communism, is a fanatical religion. It tends to subordinate not only truth but also morality and individuals to the cause. The destruction of Communism becomes an end which justifies any effective means.

Christians should not commit themselves to such a Crusade. For the same reasons that they reject religious Communism, they should also reject religious anti-Communism. Each is an idolatrous alternative to Christian faith.

The criticism also ignores the book's basic *disagreements* with Communist ideology. These disagreements are not based on right-wing *political* convictions. Such convictions may be *compatible* with Christian faith but they cannot be *derived* from Christian faith as such. The disagreements are based on specifically *Christian* convictions, and so they carry weight with left-wing Christians who are repelled by right-wing arguments. For example, one such Christian has said that the book is the most profoundly anti-Communist work that he has read.

3. A third criticism of the book is that it was written in an ivory tower, remote from situations where Communism is a life-or-death issue. It attempts to be detached and impartial and objective, but it fails to grapple with political realities in countries which, unlike Canada, have experienced Communism first-hand. How can men who have never experienced such things as the Communist take-over in Czechoslovakia or the Stalinist concentration camps think realistically about Communist theory?

In reply I want first of all to express my respect and my sympathy for the critic who *has* come through such experiences. Nevertheless, I must point out that it is easier to be dispassionate and objective concerning an evil if one has not been its victim. For example, it is easier for me to be realistic concerning capital punishment than it is for a man whose child has been brutally murdered. In relation to Communist theory, a native Canadian and a refugee from Communism are likely to differ in the same way. The 'ivory tower' involves no heroism or virtue, but it does have advantages. It is a vantage point from which one is more likely to see the full extent of the landscape, both the bad and the good. Of course, it also has serious disadvantages. The detached observer does not know the appalling details of Communist *practice* first-hand. If this book pretended to be a survey of Communist practice, the criticism would be very cogent indeed. But such a book would have to include not only the horrors of Communism but also the horrors which give rise to Communism. Such a book would have to describe not only the sufferings of our fellow-Christians and others under Communist persecution but also the sufferings of our fellow-Christians and others under oppressive regimes which are nominally Christian.

Indeed, *Communist Faith and Christian Faith* might well be criticized from a very different point of view. Communist theory would look very different to a Latin American reformer who lives in the midst of terrible poverty and corruption, and who sees in the Communist movement the only practical remedy at hand. Such a man, like a refugee from Communism, might well challenge a book written in the opulent safety and freedom of Canada. Nevertheless, in his desperation, he might fail to be realistic about Communist theory. For example, he might not reckon seriously with the fact that Communist morality sanctions any treachery, to enemy or to *ally*, as long as it genuinely furthers the Communist cause. Like a Communist refugee, though in a different way, he will find it hard to be objective about Communist theory.

4. A fourth criticism, which comes from both the political left and political right, is that the book is politically irresponsible: the book purports to give a 'basis for Christian decisions which are reasonable and faithful' in various political situations. Yet it deals only with Communist theory, ignoring Communist practice. Moreover, it ignores other fundamental

political factors in the world today: nationalistic fervour, racial hatred, technological innovation, population explosion, the Bomb.

I agree that if this book were the only basis for a Christian's political decisions the results would be disastrous. But the book does not purport to provide such a basis by itself. Only a modest hope was expressed: that, along with other works in the bibliographies, it might 'help' to provide such a basis. The bibliographies refer to various accounts of Communist theory and practice, and Christian appraisals of Communist theory and practice. The book, however, has a very limited objective: the comparison of Christian and Communist *theory*. Such a comparison is worth doing, because most studies merge theory and practice in such a way that there is no clear confrontation between Christian and Communist convictions. Such a comparison could not be made if one tried to deal with matters of Communist (and Christian) practice, let alone the many other matters which are important in the world today.

Nevertheless, it is perhaps useful here to distinguish five different ways in which Communist practice may differ from Communist theory. (1) *Insincerity*. A Communist may inwardly disbelieve the theory while nevertheless acting as if he believed it—so as to avoid punishment or to gain advancement. (2) *Self-deception*. A Communist may think that he is motivated by belief in the theory, although his real motivation is very different, for example, a lust for power. (3) *Superficiality*. A Communist may believe the theory, but only in a superficial way. It has little real influence on what he does, or even on what he *thinks* concerning what he does. (4) *Ideological conservatism*. A Communist may justify some new official practice by reference to Marxism-Leninism, but do so only because an appeal is required if the ideology is to be preserved in its coherence and authority. His appeal may be merely a cynical gesture or it may be a sincere rationalization. In neither case, however, can the new practice be justified solely by reference to official theory; new considerations have entered in. (5) *Party-line lies*. A Communist may announce a new Communist policy, not because it is actually going to be followed by the Party, but because the Communist cause will be furthered if people believe him.

In the book we did not discuss the extent to which any of the five deviations occur within particular Communist Parties. Obviously the question is extremely important.

5. A fifth criticism, from the political left, is that the book does not provide a Christian alternative to Communism. The book accepts some of the Communist's ideals for society, and expounds other ideals, but it fails to set forth any specific economic or political programme for achieving the ideals. It indicates some of the social implications of the Gospel, but it fails to build any bridge between theory and practice. Surely Communism as a plan of corporate action needs to be challenged by a Christian plan of corporate action. Surely all Christians should have a definite and agreed position concerning each important economic and political question. Only thus will the Christian ideology, the Social Gospel, encounter Communist ideology at every point.

My reply to this criticism is that it ignores or rejects the main point in the book: Christian faith cannot provide answers to *factual* questions in economics or politics; and, even in the realm of economic and political *values*, it does not rule out the possibility of disagreement between Christians who agree concerning the facts. If Christian faith became an ideology, a programme for social action, it would cease to be Christian faith. Either the programme would be elevated to a phoney position as part of God's revelation to man, or the revelation of God in Christ would be reduced to the level of a human programme.

Nevertheless, the criticism does suggest a way in which the book could be misleading. Since we stressed Christian '*options*' concerning economic and political questions, we may have given the impression that these questions are optional—that is, unimportant. Since the Christian faith itself dictates no answers to these questions, some readers might think that Christians can opt *out* of them. This is not so. Each Christian bears a responsibility to build a bridge from his Christian faith to Christian social action, even though many of his building materials cannot be quarried from his faith.

The criticism also reminds us of another point which might have been obscured: that individual Christians have a responsibility to try for some measure of agreement with other Christians concerning such matters, even though a common Christian faith does not itself ensure a common mind concerning social issues. However, it is also true that a Christian should try for some measure of political agreement with *non*-Christians. In some circumstances this may be more important.

6. So far in this postscript I have been replying to criticisms. Now I should like to *make* one: the account of Christian convictions is rather vague in several important places. Sometimes the vagueness is my fault. Sometimes it was the price of obtaining agreement in a committee. Whatever the reason, the following points seem to *me* to be in special need of further clarification and discussion:

(1) Sin is described as the 'decisive cause' of moral evil, in contrast with various 'secondary causes' (p. 30). How does a decisive cause differ from a secondary cause? By being the most important? If so, in what sense of 'most important'? Indeed, is the word 'sin' ever used rightly to refer to a *cause* of moral evil alongside other causes? If not, then perhaps it is used to say something important about the *effect*; that is, it is used to point out that moral evil includes alienation from God. Or is sin *both* the most important cause of moral evil and the most important characteristic of moral evil? All this is extremely obscure.

(2) 'God reveals himself in various ways to *all* men' (p. 33). This statement evades fundamental questions concerning natural theology or general revelation: What can non-Christians know of God? What can't they know?

(3) According to the book (p. 64), material rewards should correspond to services rendered. Not only realism but also *justice* requires this, so it is claimed; for even in a sinless society it would be just to *try* to give special rewards for special services. 'Why?', we may ask. Would it not also be

just to try to equalize rewards, or to try to proportion rewards entirely to needs? The basis of the argument here is not clear.

(4) The book indicates two different ways in which Christ comes to the Christian: through the Church and through society (pp. 101-2). On the one hand, Christ comes through Gospel, sacraments and fellow Christians. On the other hand, he comes in the needy man whom one helps and the man by whom one is helped. Are these both cases of the 'Real Presence' or do they differ in kind? Which is more important? Much of the current controversy concerning the so-called 'new theology' is focused on such questions. The book does not attempt to answer them.

(5) The book repeats the customary teaching of modern biblical theology concerning revelation: God reveals himself in mighty historical acts such as rescuing the Israelites from Egypt or punishing them by destruction and Exile (pp. 104-6). Does this mean that God revealed himself in the slaughter of the Egyptian first-born (cf. Hitler slaughtering the Jews) and in the collective punishment of a nation, including infants? If not, what does it mean?

(6) According to the book, all history will be fulfilled in the End (p. 108). Does this conviction rule out the possibility of mankind annihilating itself? If it does, is Christian faith thereby open to possible falsification in the future? If it does not, what, specifically, *does* it rule out? If nothing concerning future earthly history is ruled out, in what sense is God in 'control' of history?

(7) The book deals extensively with a traditional interpretation of the End as something in the future. Then it outlines a symbolic, non-temporal interpretation (pp. 116-7). Is the second interpretation a sheer contradiction of the first? Which interpretation is true?

(8) The book tackles a difficult and crucial problem for modern men: the morality of violent revolution (pp. 125-6). However, its presentation of a possible new doctrine concerning the 'just revolution' is brief and superficial. The problem, and related problems concerning non-violent political protests,

deserve extensive and profound study throughout the whole Christian Church.

I have noted eight places where, it seems to me, the book does not deal adequately with an important issue. This does not mean that I regret not having tried to settle each issue. It would have been silly to have grasped every theological nettle that we encountered on the way. Nevertheless, I think that readers may find it interesting to have these painful and fascinating problems pointed out in this personal postscript.

In conclusion, I should like to express my deep appreciation to the Committee on Christian Faith. It is always difficult to write for a committee. In this case, however, the difficulty was trivial compared with the benefit of so many cogent objections and illuminating suggestions. Without the Committee's ideas, the book would have been vastly inferior. Without the Committee's encouragement, it would never have been finished.

SHORT BIBLIOGRAPHY FOR STUDY GROUPS

('p' means 'paper-back')

1. **Readings in Communism**
   K. Marx and F. Engels, *On Religion,* Lawrence and Wishart, 1958.
   A. P. Mendel (ed.), *Essential Works of Marxism*, Transworld Publishers, London, 1962.

2. **Surveys of Communism**
   A. G. Meyer, *Communism,* Random House, 1963 (p).
   Edward Crankshaw, *The New Cold War, Moscow v. Pekin,* Penguin, 1963 (p).
   R. V. Daniels, *The Nature of Communism,* Vintage, 1963 (p).

3. **Christian Discussions of Communism** (in order of usefulness)
   John C. Bennett, *Christianity and Communism Today,* SCM, 1960 (p).
   Charles W. Forman (ed.), *A Christian's Handbook of Communism,* John Knox Press, Richmond, Virginia, 1964 (p).
   Alexander Miller, *The Christian Significance of Karl Marx,* SCM, 1952.
   J. M. Cameron, *Scrutiny of Marxism,* SCM, 1948.
   Johannes Hamel, *A Christian in East Germany,* SCM, 1960.
   F. Ernest Johnson, *A Vital Encounter: Christianity and Communism,* Abingdon, 1962 (p).
   Emil Brunner, *Communism, Capitalism, and Christianity,* Lutterworth, London, 1950 (p).

4. **Christian Social Ethics**
   J. C. McLelland, *The Other Six Days*, John Knox Press, Richmond, Virginia, 1961 (p).
   J. C. Bennett, *The Christian as Citizen,* Lutterworth, 1950 (p).
   Pope John XXIII, *Mater et Magistra* (Mother and Teacher) and *Pacem in Terris* (Peace on Earth).

BIBLIOGRAPHY FOR FURTHER STUDY

1. Readings in Communism

K. Marx and F. Engels, *Selected Works,* Vols. I, II, Foreign Languages Publishing House, Moscow, 1949. *Basic Writings on Politics and Philosophy,* ed. Lewis S. Feuer, Mayflower Books London 1961. (p).

K. Marx, F. Engels and V. I. Lenin, *Reader in Marxist Philosophy,* ed. H. Selsam and H. Martel, International Publishers, NY (p) (pro-Communist).

V. I. Lenin, *Imperialism,* Foreign Languages Publishing House, Moscow. *The State and Revolution,* Foreign Languages Publishing House, Moscow.

The Differences Between Comrade Togliatti and Us, Foreign Language Press, Peking, 1963.

2. Secondary Sources on Communism

R. N. Carew Hunt, *The Theory and Practice of Communism,* London, 1950 (p).

M. M. Bober, *Karl Marx's Interpretation of History,* Harvard, 1948.

Sidney Hook, *Marx and the Marxists,* Van Nostrand, London, 1955 (p).

C. Wright Mills, *The Marxists,* Transatlantic Books, London, 1962 (p).

Vernon Venable, *Human Nature: the Marxian View,* Dennis Dobson Ltd., London, 1946.

Howard Selsam, *Socialism and Ethics,* Lawrence and Wishart, London, 1949 (pro-Communist).

Robert Tucker, *Philosophy and Myth in Karl Marx,* Cambridge, 1961 (p).

Erich Fromm, *Marx's Concept of Man,* Ungar, NY, 1961 (p) (includes Marx's 1844 writings).

3. Christian Discussions on Communism

Hans-Gerhard Koch, *The Abolition of God,* SCM, 1961.

Karl Barth and Johannes Hamel, *How to Serve God in a Marxist Land,* Association Press, NY, 1959.

Katharine Hockin, *Servants of God in People's China,* SCM, 1964 (p).

Elisabeth Adler (ed.), *Pro-Existence*, SCM, 1964 (p).

Francis P. Jones, *The Church in Communist China,* Friendship Press, 1962 (p).

General Assembly of the Church of Scotland, *The Challenge of Communism,* SCM, 1952 (p); *The Church Under Communism,* SCM, 1952 (p).

Alasdair MacIntyre, *Marxism, an Interpretation,* SCM, 1953.

Henri Chambre, *Christianity and Communism,* Burns, Oates, London, 1960.

Paul Ramsey, 'Religious Aspects of Marxism', in *Nine Modern Moralists,* Prentice-Hall, 1962 (p).

D. M. Mackinnon (ed.), *Christian Faith and Communist Faith,* Macmillan, 1952.

Charles West, *Communism and the Theologians,* SCM, 1958 (a monumental theological study).

Edward Rogers, *A Christian Commentary on Communism,* Epworth, London, 1959 (p).

Leslie Dewart, *Christianity and Revolution, The Lesson of Cuba,* Herder and Herder, NY, 1963.

J. Lewis, K. Polanyi and D. K. Kitchin, *Christianity and Social Revolution,* Gollancz, London, 1935 (contains some essays by Communists).

4. Christian Social Ethics

Joseph P. Fletcher (ed.), *Christianity and Property,* Westminster, 1947.

John C. Bennett, *Christians and the State,* Scribners, NY, 1958. *Christian Faith and Political Choice,* Ryerson, Toronto, 1963.

E. Clinton Gardner, *Biblical Faith and Social Ethics,* NY, 1960.

Emil Brunner, *Justice and the Social Order,* Lutterworth, London, 1949.

5. Christian Eschatology

Daniel Day Williams, *God's Grace and Man's Hope,* NY, 1949.

John Baillie, *The Belief in Progress,* Oxford, 1950.

J. A. T. Robinson, *In the End, God,* James Clarke, London, 1950.

Karl Lowith, *Meaning in History,* Chicago, 1949.

H. Butterfield, *Christianity and History,* Fontana, 1957 (p).

Scholars will also find it helpful to consult two bibliographies:

M. Searle Bates, *A Christian's Select Bibliography on Communism,* Missionary Research Library, 3041 Broadway, New York 27, NY, 1961.

C. H. Jacquet, Jr., *Communism: a Selected and Annotated Bibliography,* National Council of the Churches of Christ in the USA, 475 Riverside Drive, New York 27, NY, 1963.

A GUIDE FOR STUDY GROUPS

PROCEDURE

How many meetings should we have?

At least four:

1. Introduction and Chapter 1
2. Chapter 2
3. Chapter 3
4. Chapter 4

Or perhaps seven:

1. Introduction and Chapter 1
2. Chapter 2, section 1
3. Chapter 2, sections 2 and 3
4. Chapter 3, section 1
5. Chapter 3, sections 2 and 3
6. Chapter 4, section 1
7. Chapter 4, sections 2 and 3

What should we read?

Every member of the group should try to read the *whole* of a chapter before any part of it is studied and discussed.

Obviously the discussion will be better if members of the group are also reading some of the books suggested in the Bibliography. Each member could read a different book.

Do we need experts?

No.

However, if a group has the good fortune to be able to call on expert resource leaders, it should do so. For example, an economist or an expert on Soviet affairs would be very helpful for the meeting on Communist convictions concerning property and economics.

What questions are relevant?

Two kinds of questions (which appear below) should be considered:

(a) Questions for *clarification*—which help members of the group to test their *understanding* of the material.

(b) Questions for *discussion*—which help members of the group to decide whether or not they *agree* with the material.

The group leader will naturally use his own discretion in using or ignoring the questions which appear below, in posing his own questions, and in encouraging initiative from within the group.

QUESTIONS

Introduction

(a) *Questions for clarification:*

1. In what ways does this booklet differ from other accounts of Christianity and Communism?
2. Why is it difficult to compare Christian faith with Communist faith?
3. Under what different circumstances do Christians confront Communists in the world today? How do the issues differ in these different situations?

(b) *Questions for discussion:*

1. Can any realistic comparison be made between the 'fruits' of Christianity and the 'fruits' of Communism? If so, how could this be done?
2. How important is the common 'core' of Communist theory in world affairs today?
3. Christians disagree considerably concerning Communism. Is this a bad thing?
4. Is it impossible for Christians and Communists to co-exist indefinitely?

Chapter 1, Communism and Christianity

(a) *Questions for clarification:*

1. What are the main similarities between Christianity and Communism as historical movements?
2. What are the main differences between Christianity and Communism as historical movements?

(b) *Questions for discussion:*

1. What is a heresy? Is Communism a Christian heresy?
2. How do you explain the missionary zeal of Communism?

Chapter 2, Section (1), What does the Communist Believe about Nature, Man and God?

(a) *Questions for clarification:*

1. What is meant by 'forces of production'?
2. What is meant by the 'conflict between the forces of production and the relations of production'?

3. What do Communists mean by the folowing terms:

'socialism'	'superstructure'
'communism'	'materialism'
'idealism'	'opium of the people'
'ideology'	

4. Why is anti-religious propaganda important for Communists? Why isn't it all-important?

(b) *Questions for discussion:*
1. Communists hold that economic factors are decisive in history. Do you agree? If you disagree, then what factors *are* decisive? Are *any* factors decisive?
2. Do any of the Communist criticisms of religion apply to the Church as you know it today?
3. Which elements in Communist atheism are distinctively *Communist*? Which are common to Western atheists generally?
4. Why is atheism evil? Is atheism more evil than injustice?
5. Could historical materialism be revised so as to cease being atheistic?

Chapter 2, section 2, What does the Christian believe about Nature, Man and God?

(a) *Questions for clarification:*
1. In what sense is Christian faith 'materialistic'?
2. What place does scientific advance have in the Christian view of nature and man?
3. What are the main points in Christian teaching concerning sin?
4. How does Christian motivation differ from that of unbelievers who serve their fellow-man?

(b) *Questions for discussion:*
1. What place is there for 'other-worldliness' in the Christian faith?
2. Where, if anywhere, do science and Christian faith conflict today?
3. Is sin the only cause of moral evil in individuals and societies?
4. How does the Christian insight concerning 'ideology' differ from the Communist?

5. Does the parable of the Last Judgment (Matt. 25. 31-46) conflict with the doctrine of justification by faith?
6. In what sense is an atheist a 'child of God'?

Chapter 2, section 3, Commentary

(a) *Questions for clarification:*

1. Do Communist explanations of the origin of religious beliefs show anything concerning whether these beliefs are true?
2. What is the main defect in Communist arguments for atheism?
3. What is the difference between theoretical atheism and practical atheism?
4. What are the Christian answers to the four Communist criticisms of religion:
   (i) Religion is unrealistic idealism.
   (ii) Man creates God in his own image.
   (iii) Religion is illusion and ideology.
   (iv) Religion is pseudo-science.

(b) *Questions for discussion:*

1. Does it matter to Christian faith whether or not the world had a beginning?
2. Is it un-Christian to have faith in man?
3. Are the most important changes in history produced by ideas and individuals or by economic forces?
4. 'Christian faith, rightly understood, is not a faith in a "God of the gaps" in science.' If this is true, does it mean that science might one day explain everything and yet still leave room for belief in a God who *acts* in the world?
5. Do you agree with Brunner that, 'where there are people permeated with the Spirit of Christ, right relationships, laws and arrangements always follow'?

Chapter 3, Section 1, What Does the Communist Believe about Property and Economics?

(a) *Questions for clarification:*

1. What do Communists mean by the following terms:

'exploitation'	'dictatorship of the proletariat'
'social ownership'	'public self-government'
'imperialism'	'classless society'

2. According to Communists, what is the fundamental contradiction of capitalism, and in what ways is it manifested?

3. Why do Communists attach so much importance to educating masses in Marxism-Leninism?
4. How does the New Programme plan a transition from the socialist principle 'to each according to his work' to the Communist principle 'to each according to his need'?
5. What changes in human beings do Communists expect under communism?

(b) *Questions for discussion:*

1. The New Programme claims that capitalist exploitation of the working people is 'continuously increasing', and it rejects various objections to this claim. Do you agree or disagree? What evidence have you?
2. The New Programme claims that Communist socialism releases productive forces which are inhibited under capitalism. Do you agree or disagree? What evidence have you?
3. The New Programme claims that 'the expropriated masses have no other prospect of acquiring property than the revolutionary establishment of the social ownership of means of production' Do you agree or disagree? What evidence have you?
4. The New Programme claims that under 'socialism' it is right and necessary to have a 'dictatorship of the Proletariat'. It also claims that this coercive state will wither away under 'communism'. Discuss these claims.
5. The New Programme lists a number of elements in the ideal communist society of the future. Which of these, if any, is likely to become a reality?
6. Discuss the questions of non-Communist economists which appear on page 57.

Chapter 3, Section 2, What Does the Christian Believe about Property and Economics?

(a) *Questions for clarification:*

1. Why is the distinction between 'fact' and 'value' important in considering the notion of a 'Christian economics'?
2. What do Christians mean by the following terms:

'detachment'	'partiality to the poor'
'stewardship'	'fellowship-love'

3. What criteria are listed by the study booklet in relation to

production and to distribution? Which criteria are given priority?

4. What are the main features of 'economic democracy'?
5. Why are the 'side-effects' of an economic system important?

(b) *Questions for discussion:*

1. Is it unChristian to enjoy a sumptuous meal in a world where millions of people are starving?
2. Is the 'communism' of New Testament Christians and of later Christian communities completely irrelevant to problems concerning the economic policies of a modern nation-state?
3. 'As long as men lack the elementary necessities of life, excessive wealth is unjust, regardless of how it has been acquired.' Do you agree or disagree?
4. 'Not only prudence but also *justice* requires that some men should receive more than others for their services to the community.' Do you agree or disagree?
5. In relation to producer's goods, the primary issue is not ownership but what we shall call 'economic democracy'. Do you agree or disagree?
6. Is the study booklet realistic in what it says about the right to work in relation to automation?
7. To what extent does our own economic system have beneficial (or evil) side-effects on persons? How does it compare with the Russian economic system in these respects?

Chapter 3, Commentary

Questions for Clarification and Discussion:

1. Which of the Christian disagreements with Communism (concerning property and economics) seem to you to be sound? Would you add any more?
2. Which of the Christian agreements with Communism (concerning property and economics) seem to you to be sound? Would you add any more?
3. Some people hold that although a Communist regime would be an unjustifiable tragedy in England or Canada it might be the best available system for a country which is economically underdeveloped and politically backward. Do you agree or disagree? What evidence have you?

4. Can you suggest a situation in which Christians might agree concerning the relevant economic facts and Christian criteria, but disagree concerning *priorities* of criteria?

Chapter 4, Section 1, What Does the Communist Believe about History, Hope and Morality?

(a) *Questions for clarification:*

1. What is the relation between the Communist conviction that history is 'dialectical' and Communist assurance concerning the future?
2. What do Communists mean when they say that theory depends on practice?
3. What are the main elements in the Communist idea of 'freedom'?
4. 'Communists live during a period when two epochs overlap.' What does this mean?
5. What do Communists mean by 'democratic centralism'?
6. What is the one criterion for Communist morality? What is the role of the Party in applying this criterion?
7. What do Communists mean by 'liberalism', 'objectivism' and 'idealism'? Why do Communists regard these as dangers?

(b) *Questions for discussion:*

1. Communists believe that communism is inevitable and yet they also strive to bring it in. Is this inconsistent? (Is Christian belief in 'predestination' and in 'working out our own salvation' at all similar to this?)
2. Communists see in history a pattern of *dialectical progress.* To what extent, if any, does this correspond with the facts of history?
3. Communists claim that economic 'freedom' will eventually bring both political freedom and freedom from crime. Do you agree or disagree? What evidence have you?
4. Communists hold that the Russian Revolution of 1917 was the turning-point of human history. How important do you think it was?
5. Communists claim that morality is not a transcendent reality, but a human creation which reflects class interests. To what extent is this true?
6. What do you think is the worst defect in Communist morality?

Chapter 4, Section 2, What Does the Christian Believe about History, Hope and Morality?

(a) *Questions for clarification:*

1. What does it mean to 'participate in God's historical activity in Jesus Christ'? Why is the belief that Jesus is still alive so important in relation to this?
2. What was the two-fold pattern in the sacred history of Israel?
3. 'Christians believe that they live in the period of overlap between the Old Age and the New.' What does this mean?
4. What is the difference between Christian hope concerning the End and hopes for future progress in history?
5. Why do Christians today face a question concerning human progress which was not faced by Christians in the New Testament times?
6. What are the four Christian principles for political action?
7. What is the relation between the idea of a 'just war' and the idea of a 'just revolution'?

(b) *Questions for discussion:*

1. Have you had any personal experience of the presence of the risen Jesus Christ? How important is such an experience?
2. According to the Old Testament, God was active in the affairs of nations. Do you believe that he is active in international affairs today? If so, in what way?
3. Discuss each argument in the debate between Christian 'optimists' and Christian 'pessimists'.
4. Do you think that AD 2000 will be any nearer to the End than AD 1965 is?
5. Does your Christian hope concerning the End rule out the possibility that mankind may completely annihilate itself?
6. Does Christian 'realism' differ from the realism of unbelievers who have a fairly pessimistic view of human nature?
7. Which actions, if any, are intrinsically wrong? On what basis do you distinguish these from other actions which are evil, but permissible in war or revolution?
8. Is it ever right for Christians to take part in violent revolution?

Chapter 4, Commentary

(a) *Questions for clarification:*

1. What is the fundamental Christian disagreement with Communism concerning moral evil?

261.73
EV9

37392

2. Why is it un-Christian to try to 'master' history?
3. What is the Christian position concerning 'idealism', 'objectivism' and 'liberalism' (as Communists define these terms)?
4. In what ways is Communism 'utopian'?
5. The quotation from Charles West compresses many thoughts into a few sentences. Consider each sentence carefully, asking 'What does he mean by this?' and 'What would be an example of this?'

(b) *Questions for discussion:*

1. To what extent is it realistic to say that contemporary Communism is a 'religion'? Is there any evidence that Communism may become less militant and dogmatic?
2. Is it un-Christian to regard death as a 'tragic shadow'?
3. To what extent are Christians today guilty of religious pride, religious fanaticism or religious utopianism? Do you see any evidence of a danger that Christians may turn anti-Communism into a religion?
4. Do you accept the 'agreements with Communism' which are suggested? Would you add any others?
5. Discuss the quotations from Miller and Brunner with which the chapter ends.

3 4711 00175 4664